Stages of Change and the
Group Treatment of Batterers

National Institute of Justice (NIJ), Pamela C. Alexander

The author(s) shown below used Federal funds provided by the U.S. Department of Justice and prepared the following final report:

Document Title:	Stages of Change and the Group Treatment of Batterers
Author:	Pamela C. Alexander
Document No.:	228004
Date Received:	August 2009
Award Number:	2004-WG-BX-0001

This report has not been published by the U.S. Department of Justice. To provide better customer service, NCJRS has made this Federally-funded grant final report available electronically in addition to traditional paper copies.

Stages of Change and the Group Treatment of Batterers

(2004-WG-BX-0001)

Final Report to National Institute of Justice

March 31, 2007

Pamela C. Alexander

Wellesley Centers for Women

Abstract

A Stages of Change (SOC) treatment approach, supplemented by Motivational Interviewing techniques (Miller & Rollnick, 2002), was compared with a standard cognitive-behavioral therapy gender-reeducation (CBTGR) approach for its effectiveness in reducing men's violence against their partners. A total of 528 male batterers from the Montgomery County, Maryland Abused Persons Program were randomly assigned to 49 26-week groups in either the SOC or CBTGR condition. English-speaking and Spanish-speaking groups were conducted in both treatment conditions. While certain differences emerged between English- and Spanish-speakers and their partners, men in the two treatment conditions (and their partners) did not differ with respect to demographics, lifetime violence, psychopathology, multiple admissions, histories of trauma, or source of referral as a function of their assignment to different treatment conditions. Differences between women who were successfully contacted for follow-up and those who were not were minimal, indicating the generalizability of victim follow-up reports.

Self-reported aggression at post-treatment was unrelated to treatment condition. However, based on victim follow-up reports, the SOC curriculum was more effective than standard treatment in reducing women's risk for physical aggression, especially among English-speakers. The SOC condition was particularly effective for first-time offenders, for men who were court-ordered to treatment and for men in an earlier underlying stage of change. On the other hand, the SOC condition was no more effective than the CBTGR condition in reducing the violence of men with multiple admissions, suggesting the need for warning their victims and for using a coordinated community response. The SOC condition was also not effective for men who were self-referred to treatment, presumably because it did not quickly provide the anger-management and conflict resolution skills these men were seeking. The two treatments did not differ in rates of attendance (either number of sessions attended or treatment completion), working alliance or group cohesion. Different predictors of attendance did emerge between the two conditions. Moreover, blind ratings of audiotapes of sessions significantly differentiated the two conditions.

Specific treatment considerations for Spanish-speakers were explored as was the necessity of attending to the trauma histories of both men and their partners. Finally, the reactions of therapists working with the SOC curriculum were described as were the limitations of this study and suggestions for future research. It was concluded that within the context of these limitations, this project allowed a fairly rigorous but also realistic test of the usefulness of SOC treatment in reducing men's risk for violence.

Executive Summary

Introduction

Research suggests that the effectiveness of group treatment for batterers is marginal at best (Babcock, Green, & Robie, 2004). In fact, neither a Duluth-based group treatment format (cf., Davis & Taylor, 1997) nor a cognitive-behavioral group treatment format (cf., Dunford, 2000) has been found to be more effective than no treatment at all (i.e., community service, probation or no treatment). One reason is that standard treatment formats fail in their efforts to engage resistant batterers, who normally comprise most court-ordered offenders. For example, the typical stance of the Duluth model is to confront the batterer's denial, although confrontational approaches with other resistant populations (such as substance abusers) have been proven to lead to negative outcomes (Lambert & Bergin, 1994; Miller, 1985). Moreover, the use of skills-training and other behavioral techniques in cognitive-behavioral approaches assumes a well-motivated client (Daniels & Murphy, 1997).

In contrast, the Transtheoretical Model of Change (TTM) appears to be particularly applicable to a resistant population. As described by Prochaska and DiClemente (1984), the TTM (or Stages of Change approach) assumes that all individuals go through a series of stages, ranging from precontemplation (characterized by denial or minimization) to contemplation (characterized by dawning awareness of the seriousness of the problem) to preparation (characterized by intention to change) to action (characterized by active steps to change the behavior) to maintenance (characterized by active monitoring to assure that the behavior does not resume). Research also suggests that different types of intervention are appropriate for individuals in different stages of change, with experiential and consciousness-raising activities more appropriate for individuals in an earlier stage of change and behavioral interventions more useful for individuals in a later stage of change. This model has been applied descriptively and proscriptively to batterer populations (Daniels & Murphy, 1997; Levesque, Gelles, & Velicer, 2000; Scott, 2004; Scott & Wolfe, 2003). Moreover, it is also consistent with the use of Motivational Interviewing techniques (focused on highlighting discrepancies between a client's values and behaviors) and therapist stance (characterized by reflective listening, affirmation of the client's freedom of choice and attention to the client's readiness to change), which have been used quite successfully with substance abusers (Miller & Rollnick, 2002). However, a randomized assessment of its effectiveness with batterers has not yet been conducted.

Therefore, it was the goal of this project to compare the effectiveness of a 26-week stages of change (SOC) group treatment approach with a standard cognitive-behavioral therapy gender-reeducation (CBTGR) group treatment approach; to assess potential mediators of change; to conduct analyses on individual readiness to change as a moderator of treatment condition in predicting outcomes; to conduct exploratory analyses comparing the effectiveness of these two approaches in Spanish-speaking groups; and to assess the integrity of the two treatments with respect to therapist adherence. The outcomes of interest included a man's desistance from violence (as assessed by his self-reported scores of violent behavior at the end of treatment, and more importantly, his partner's report of his psychological and physical aggression toward her at follow-up), indicators of increased involvement (including the number of sessions attended, therapist and client ratings of working alliance and client ratings of group cohesion), and his assumption of responsibility over the course of treatment (as assessed by a change in his underlying stage of change). Other characteristics purported to potentially interact with treatment effectiveness such as multiple admissions and source of referral were also assessed as was therapist adherence to the respective treatment condition. This project was conducted at the Montgomery County, Maryland Abused Persons Program.

Description of Treatment Formats

The general therapist stance characterizing the SOC condition was based on a Motivational Interviewing model, including the use of open-ended questions, asking about both positive and negative aspects of the problem, listening reflectively, being willing to revise these reflections upon clarification from the client, highlighting discrepancies between clients' values and their behavior, affirming a client's efforts to change, and reflecting upon his ambivalence to change. The first 14 sessions of the curriculum made use of consciousness-raising and other experiential exercises more germane to individuals in an earlier stage of change, while the final 12 sessions focused on exercises more characteristic of individuals in a later stage of change (including typical behavioral interventions such as the use of time-out strategies, communication skills, and other counter conditioning and reinforcement management techniques). The therapist stance characterizing the CBTGR condition emphasized presenting reasons why clients should change, focusing on client behaviors, encouraging a change of controlling and abusive behavior, and confronting clients' minimization, denial and justification of their abuse. This curriculum made use of behavioral techniques from the very beginning of the group (including time-out strategies and anger journals).

Sample

The sample consisted of a total of 528 batterers, 96.1% of whom were court-ordered to treatment. They were randomly assigned to a total of 19 English-speaking groups in the SOC condition (with a total of 200 men), 16 English-speaking groups in the CBTGR condition (with a total of 175 men), 4 Spanish-speaking groups in the SOC condition (with a total of 47 men), and 10 Spanish-speaking groups in the CBTGR condition (with a total of 106 men). Therapists only led groups in one condition in order to maximize adherence to that treatment condition. Comparisons were made to assess the comparability of men in the two different treatment conditions across two different languages spoken. (Men were only considered to have been assigned to a particular treatment format if they attended at least one session of that treatment condition.)

While certain differences emerged in the demographic makeup of English- and Spanish-speakers and their partners, men in the two treatment conditions (and their partners) did not differ with respect to demographics. Similarly, although Spanish-speakers were more likely to minimize the extent of their lifetime violence toward their partners, neither they nor English-speakers differed with respect to their level of violence severity (based on self-report and partner-report) or perceived dangerousness as a function of assignment to treatment condition. Spanish-speakers scored significantly higher than English-speakers on a measure of antisocial behavior and significantly lower on self-reported drug use; however, neither they nor English-speakers differed on these variables as a function of assignment to treatment condition. Overall, 10.5% of the men in this study had been admitted to the program or to groups multiple times; however, men did not differ in their likelihood of having multiple admissions as a function of treatment conditions. While both men and their female partners reported significant histories of childhood trauma and Spanish-speakers reported less childhood trauma, individuals did not vary in their trauma history as a function of their assignment to different treatment conditions. Overall, 96.1% of men had been court-mandated to treatment and 3.9% were self-referred; English- and Spanish-speakers did not differ with respect to their source of referral. Therefore, while certain systematic differences emerged between English- and Spanish-speakers, differences in the men and their partners did not emerge as a function of the men's assignment to the two different treatment conditions. The comparability of these groups thus argued for the success of the random assignment.

Treatment Outcomes

Desistance from Violence. *Men's Self-Reports.* Men's post-treatment CTS data were highly skewed (not surprising given the low frequency of reported behavior). Therefore, logistic regression analysis was used to assess the effect of treatment condition and language spoken on men's self-reported psychological or physical aggression at post-treatment. Results of these analyses were not significant.

Victim Follow-up Reports. Because of a variability of time between intake and men's assignment to a group, victim partner follow-ups at six and twelve-months post-intake were combined, covarying for the actual length of time between a man's actual startdate for a group and the victim follow-up. The results of logistic regression analyses suggested that a woman was significantly less likely to report physical aggression at follow-up if her partner had been enrolled in the SOC condition, especially for English-speaking individuals. (Treatment type was not associated with different levels of psychological aggression or injury at follow-up.) Paired comparison t-tests indicated a significant reduction overall in psychological aggression, although this did not vary with treatment condition. Moreover, a woman's increased risk for physical aggression and injury at follow-up was associated with the man's lack of treatment compliance and having had multiple admissions to the APP. First-time offenders were significantly less likely to perpetrate injury against their partner if they had been enrolled in the SOC condition, while men with multiple admissions did not respond differentially to treatment. There was a trend for self-referred men to respond less favorably to the SOC condition, as indicated by their partners' reports of physical aggression at follow-up. There was also evidence of a woman's increased vulnerability for injury at follow-up as a function of her report of having witnessed domestic violence as a child. Finally, comparisons were made between women who were successfully contacted for follow-up and those who were not, with evidence of only minimal differences, suggesting that results of victim follow-ups were generalizable to the sample overall.

Men's Assumption of Responsibility. Structural equation modeling was used to develop a unidimensional solution reflecting one's underlying stage of change at intake, allowing the comparison of men's post-treatment responses on the stage of change measure with their initial underlying stage of change. Analyses suggested that neither treatment type nor language spoken predicted change in growth from intake to post-treatment on this measure of stage of change. On the other hand, the results of a regression analysis suggested that a lack of acknowledgement at intake of one's aggression was predictive of a greater degree of change, while the victim's minimization of the impact of her partner's violence was predictive of less change in his underlying stage of change.

Attendance. The number of sessions attended was greater in Spanish-speakers than English-speakers, but there was no overall effect of treatment condition on attendance. With respect to the categorical variable of treatment completion (defined as attendance of at least 75%), 21.4% of individuals who attended at least one session failed to complete treatment. Treatment completion did not vary with type of treatment. Separate regression analyses were conducted for the two treatment types to assess differential predictors of attendance. For the CBTGR condition, number of sessions attended was positively predicted by employment and borderline traits. For the SOC condition, number of sessions attended was positively predicted by age and having been court-mandated to treatment. These results highlighted the relevance of lifestyle instability factors (Cadsky et al., 1996) for both treatment conditions, internal distress for motivating men's involvement in the CBTGR condition and court sanctions for motivating their involvement in the SOC condition. Results of a MANOVA suggested that generally violent antisocial individuals were less likely to successfully complete treatment in the SOC condition.

Working Alliance and Group Cohesion. Therapist and client reports of working alliance and client reports of group cohesion were significantly higher among Spanish-speakers than English-speakers, but were related to neither type of treatment nor to desistance from violence.

Interaction of Initial Stage of Change with Group Treatment on Outcomes. Initial stage of change interacted with treatment to predict a victim's report of physical aggression. Namely, partners of men in an earlier initial stage of change reported less physical aggression when the men had been assigned to the SOC condition, and partners of men in a later stage of change reported less physical aggression when the men had been assigned to the CBTGR condition.

Therapist Adherence. Assessment of therapist adherence was conducted by a rater who was blind to the treatment condition and listened to randomly selected audiotapes from the groups. The audiotapes were rated on general but unique counselor behaviors associated with each treatment condition (for the CBTGR condition, adopting the role of the expert, confronting clients about their abusive behavior, presenting reasons why clients should change, appealing to external authority to help clients see why they should change, focusing on client behaviors, and encouraging a change of controlling and abusive behavior; for the SOC condition, encouraging reflection, focusing on clients' values and motivations, expressing empathy for clients' experience, using open-ended questions, briefly summarizing clients' responses and exploring further, and making reflective statements). Cronbach's alpha for these scales was .889, and the two treatment conditions were significantly differentiated by the ratings on the scales.

Discussion

Overall, the comparability of men and their partners across treatment types argued for the ultimate success of random assignment in this study. The strongest findings emerged with respect to victim follow-up reports which, as opposed to self-reports at post-treatment, were completely unrelated to whether or not a man completed treatment and thus, constituted a more valid test of the efficacy of treatment.

Victim follow-up reports suggested that the SOC curriculum was more effective than standard treatment in reducing women's risk for physical aggression at follow-up. The effectiveness of the SOC condition was particularly striking among first-time offenders, among men who were court-ordered to treatment and among men in an earlier underlying stage of change, effects all consistent with hypotheses generated by the Transtheoretical Model of Change. On the other hand, the SOC condition was no more effective than the CBTGR condition in reducing the violence of men with multiple admissions, suggesting the need for adequately warning the victims of these men and for making optimal use of a coordinated community response. The SOC condition was also not effective for men who were self-referred to treatment, presumably because it did not quickly provide the anger-management and conflict resolution skills these men were seeking. Psychological aggression significantly decreased but was not eliminated in partners of men in either condition.

Suggestions were made with regard to the importance of group dynamics, specific treatment considerations for Spanish-speakers, and the necessity of attending to the trauma histories of both men and their partners. Finally, the reactions of therapists to working in the SOC condition were explored as were limitations of this study. It was concluded that within the context of these limitations, this project allowed a fairly rigorous but also realistic test of the usefulness of SOC treatment in reducing men's risk for violence.

Stages of Change and the Group Treatment of Batterers

Criminal courts have increasingly begun to rely on court-mandated treatment for domestic violence (DV) offenders. However, the success of these programs has not been overwhelming. In a meta-analysis of the outcome studies on batterer intervention programs (Babcock, Green, & Robie, 2004), there were no differences in effect sizes in comparing Duluth gender re-education model versus cognitive-behavioral type interventions. Overall, effects due to treatment were in the small range ($d = .18$), meaning that the current interventions have a minimal impact on reducing recidivism beyond the effect of being arrested. As an alternative, it was the purpose of this project to: 1) compare the effectiveness of a 26-week stages of change (SOC) group treatment approach with a standard cognitive-behavioral therapy gender-reeducation group (CBTGR) treatment approach; 2) assess whether observed changes in behavior are mediated by greater involvement in the program, as measured by increased attendance, working alliance and group cohesion; 3) assess individual readiness to change as a moderator of treatment condition in predicting outcomes; 4) conduct exploratory analyses comparing the effectiveness of these two approaches in Spanish-speaking groups; and 5) assess the integrity of the two treatments with respect to therapist adherence. The following review of the literature provides justification for this study.

Review of Relevant Literature

Perspectives Underlying Batterer Treatment Programs

While other approaches to batterer treatment have also been espoused, the feminist educational approach (i.e., the Duluth model) and the cognitive-behavioral model are the two primary models of abuser intervention programs in North America. The Duluth model (Pence & Paymar, 1983) uses the Power and Control Wheel to show how DV results from a man's attempt to reestablish his power within a household when he feels his dominance is threatened (Healey, Smith, & O'Sullivan, 1998). Confrontation of batterers appears to be an essential component of the Duluth model (Dutton & Corvo, 2006; Healey et al., 1998).

The cognitive behavioral (CBT) approach focuses on the abuser's beliefs and assumptions that lead to his misinterpretation of his partner's behavior and to his justification of his own violent behavior. This model proposes that violent behavior exists as a function of social learning from childhood or current circumstances and is maintained to the extent that it is reinforced. Batterers are taught to restructure their beliefs and "self-talk" leading to violence, using techniques such as relaxation training, conflict-resolution skills and communication skills. This approach typically incorporates feminist perspectives on DV, viewing violence in families as heavily influenced by gender beliefs and roles transmitted by the family and community. The use of confrontation as an intervention strategy is also prevalent in CBT approaches with batterers (Chang & Saunders, 2002; McCloskey, Sitaker, Grigsby, & Malloy, 2003). Moreover, as noted by Gondolf (1997b) in his review of court-ordered batterer intervention programs, "some semblance of convergence currently exists in what might be termed a gender-based, cognitive-behavioral modality. Men are confronted with the consequences of their behavior, held responsible for their abuse, have their rationalizations and excuses confronted, and are taught alternative behaviors and reactions." (p. 85). Therefore, distinctions in principle between these two perspectives are not nearly so apparent in their practice (Babcock et al., 2004). The next section consists of a brief review of research on the effectiveness of batterer intervention programs.

The Effectiveness of Batterer Treatment Programs

In 2004, Babcock et al. conducted a meta-analysis of 22 studies looking at the effectiveness of abuser intervention programs (primarily Duluth-model or CBT) relative to no-treatment. They noted that only five studies consisted of true experimental designs using random assignment of batterers to different conditions (including no-treatment). Of these five studies (Davis, Taylor, & Maxwell, 2001; Dunford, 1998; 2000; Feder & Forde, 1999; Ford & Regoli, 1993; Palmer, Brown, & Barrera, 1992), random assignment was compromised in two, the Navy study (Dunford, 1998, 2000) was not representative of the overall population of batterers, and Palmer et al. (1992) was limited by a small sample size. Based on the inclusion of these experimental designs as well as additional quasi-experimental designs, Babcock et al. determined that the overall effect size of batterer intervention programs relative to no-treatment was in the "small" range, with even smaller effect sizes observed in the five experimental studies. Namely, based on partner report at follow-up, there was only a 5% decrease in violence that was attributable to treatment, suggesting that the success rate of current batterer treatment programs is more similar to the very modest success rates of rehabilitation of adult prisoners than to psychotherapy in general. Babcock et al. also noted that there were no significant differences between the effectiveness of Duluth-model and CBT interventions.

In their review of batterer intervention programs, Davis and Taylor (1998) summarized methodological issues that, in most studies, preclude any legitimate conclusions about the effectiveness of treatment including exclusive reliance upon official reports of violence which tend to underestimate the recurrence of violence in a relationship, the use of short follow-up intervals, inadequate power to detect differences between treated and untreated participants, low response rates in the follow-up of partners and problems with attrition. They concluded that only a randomized design would offer definitive proof of the effectiveness of a particular treatment either relative to no treatment or to another treatment format. Gondolf (2001) disagreed with the assessment that only randomized designs are useful and noted that his longitudinal evaluation of four treatment programs has provided evidence of clearly promising results. He further noted that even small effect sizes may be an adequate endorsement of a treatment program.

Prediction of Recidivism

In addition to comparing the effectiveness of a treatment program to either no-treatment or to another treatment format, much research has looked at individual predictors of recidivism. Among the factors found to be most predictive of reassault is generalized aggression, including personality disorders characterized by high anger, impulsivity or behavioral instability (Cattaneo & Goodman, 2003; Grann & Wedin, 2002; Hilton & Harris, 2005; Stalans, Yarnold, Seng, Olson, & Repp, 2004). Psychological abuse at pretreatment has been found to be an important predictor of recidivism (Cattaneo & Goodman, 2003; Hilton & Harris, 2005; Murphy, Morrel, Elliott, & Neavins, 2003) as has minimization or denial of the DV (Grann & Wedin, 2002), substance abuse (Hilton & Harris, 2005; Murphy et al., 2003), treatment noncompliance (Cattaneo & Goodman, 2003; Hilton & Harris, 2005; Stalans et al., 2004) and partners' assessment of risk (Goodman, Dutton, & Bennett, 2000; Heckert & Gondolf, 2004). On the other hand, some researchers have not found that many of these variables predict reassault (Kingsnorth, 2006), others disagree about the direction of effects of variables such as severe violence (Cattaneo & Goodman, 2003; Grann & Wedin, 2002), and others have noted that it is difficult to predict recidivism (Hendricks, Werner, Shipway, & Turinetti, 2006).

Attrition from Batterer Intervention Programs

One major problem to be considered in the evaluation of batterer intervention programs
is the large rates of attrition observed in most intervention programs, with attrition typically
ranging from 50 to 75% overall (Daly & Pelowski, 2000). The range of attrition after treatment
starts is even larger with Chang and Saunders (2002) reporting a range of 14 to 56% and Buttell
and Pike (2002) reporting a range of 40 to 60%. Demographic variables reported to be
associated with attrition include unemployment (Daly, Power & Gondolf, 2001; Taft, Murphy,
Elliott & Keaser, 2001), a younger age (Chang & Saunders, 2002), race (McCloskey, Sitaker,
Grigsby, & Malloy, 2003; Taft et al., 2001), and less education (Daly et al., 2001). Other
important predictors include antisocial personality (Chang & Saunders, 2002), self-referral (Daly
et al., 2001; Gerlock, 2001; Taft et al., 2001), substance abuse (Daly et al., 2001), and not living
with a partner (McCloskey et al., 2003). Cadsky, Hanson, Crawford and Lalonde (1996)
proposed that there are two main reasons for attrition – lifestyle instability (accounting for some
of the demographic variables above) and an incongruence between the clients' perceived needs
and the treatment approach. While Rooney and Hanson (2001) found evidence of the
importance of lifestyle instability in predicting attrition, they did not find that motivation
predicted in-program attrition. Finally, consistent with Cadsky et al.'s (1996) notion of
client/treatment congruence, Chang and Saunders (2002) found different predictors of attrition
for different types of treatment groups, suggesting that the match between the client and the
treatment may not only predict reduction of violence but also attrition.

Not only is the attrition of batterers from treatment programs an obvious practical
limitation of service delivery, but it also interferes with the evaluation of programs. An
assessment of the overall effectiveness of treatment relative to no-treatment often utilizes an
"intention to treat" approach (comparing men who were assigned to a treatment condition
whether or not they attended even one session). However, as Gondolf (2001; 2004) has noted,
attributing the reassault rate of men who never even attended a single session to that type of
treatment is highly misleading. Moreover, programs are highly arbitrary in their definition of
what constitutes a drop-out (Buttell & Pike, 2002; Daly et al., 2001; McCloskey et al., 2003).
Therefore, whether the goal of the evaluation is to assess the effectiveness of treatment relative
to no-treatment or whether the goal is to compare the effectiveness of two distinct types of
treatment, it is essential to use a dose approach regarding treatment. It should be noted that an
evaluation of dose response is not inconsistent with random assignment, especially given that it
also allows an evaluation of the influence of the treatment on the construct of attrition itself.

Individual Differences in Response to Treatment

One factor that clearly emerges from the literature reviewed above is that batterers are
not a homogeneous group and that individual differences are important factors in predicting both
recidivism and attrition from treatment programs. Thus, it is likely that many potentially
significant differences between treatment conditions have gone undetected by failing to consider
individual differences among group members. Several studies have highlighted the importance
of individual differences when evaluating the effectiveness of treatment. For example, while
Saunders' (1996) feminist-cognitive-behavioral format was not found to differ overall from a
process-psychodynamic group format, batterer personality (assessed at intake) did interact
significantly with treatment condition. Namely, more dependent abusers were more likely to
profit from the process group format whereas more antisocial abusers were more likely to benefit

from the cognitive-behavioral group format. Similarly, while Brannen and Rubin (1996) did not find any significant differences between a couples cognitive-behavioral educational group format and a gender-specific group intervention in which DV offenders participated in a Duluth model group and their partners participated in empowerment groups, they did find that batterers with a history of alcohol abuse were more likely to benefit from the couples approach than from the individual group approach. Another key individual difference that may be relevant to predicting batterers' response to treatment is the degree to which they acknowledge or deny their abusive behavior.

Difficulty of Engaging the Resistant Batterer

A salient characteristic of DV offenders referred for court-ordered treatment is their denial and minimization of their violent behavior (Malloy, McCloskey, & Monford, 1999; Scalia, 1994). For example, Cadsky et al. (1996) noted that although patient compliance is a problem for almost all forms of therapy, treatment programs for male batterers face special concerns, given that the motivation for batterers to attend treatment is usually external (e.g., court-order or pressure from one's partner). Many batterers do not see themselves as having a problem with violence and, even when acknowledging that they are abusive, they may frame it in terms of a normal reaction to their partner's provocative behavior, thus obviating their ability or willingness to benefit from traditional group interventions.

Traditionally, the strategy for addressing this denial has been to adopt a confrontational approach, in order to reeducate participants or to challenge them to accept responsibility for their own behavior. However, as Murphy and Baxter (1997) have pointed out, batterers' denial and rationalization of behavior may be important in the maintenance of self-esteem and thus, may not respond to direct confrontation. Instead, "highly confrontational interventions . . . may reinforce the client's view that relationships are inevitably grounded in coercion and control, rather than in understanding, trust, and support" (p. 609). Empirical literature with other populations and other treatment modalities concludes that, in addition to being ineffective, confrontational approaches frequently lead to other negative outcomes (Gurman & Kniskern, 1978; Lambert & Bergin, 1994; Miller, 1985). Given that the risk for a negative outcome appears to be especially relevant to those of very low self-esteem and lower social status (Kaplan, 1982; Lambert & Bergin, 1994), abusers may be particularly unresponsive or even at risk for deterioration in the face of unbridled or harsh confrontation. The additional danger, of course, is that the batterer's negative experience within a group setting may translate into increased retribution against his partner.

Therefore, it is likely that at least some of the demonstrated ineffectiveness of batterer intervention programs using the Duluth model may be due to the philosophy of that treatment – namely, to confront directly the apparent denial of the perpetrator. While cognitive-behavioral approaches tend to be more collaborative in their stance toward the batterer, they are plagued by a different problem that also precludes engaging the resistant abuser – namely, their use of skills-training and other techniques assumes a well-motivated client (Daniels & Murphy, 1997). In either case, an understanding of how behavior change occurs and the means by which unmotivated clients can be engaged in this process of behavior change seems warranted. The transtheoretical model, developed for understanding the change process in substance abusers (another group characterized by denial), may be equally applicable to DV offenders.

Transtheoretical Model of Change

As articulated by Prochaska and DiClemente (1984), the transtheoretical model (TTM) assumes that all individuals go through a series of stages before a change in behavior is ever accomplished. Initially, individuals in a stage of precontemplation may either deny the behavior, minimize it, or attribute its cause to someone else. If seen in treatment, it is as a result of pressure from others (Prochaska, DiClemente, & Norcross, 1992). In the contemplation stage, they begin to acknowledge the problem's existence and negative effect, but are still not actively trying to change the behavior. In the preparation stage, they are thinking more clearly about what they can do to alter the behavior. In the action stage, they are actually focused on making behavior change and are taking active steps to alter the behavior. However, action cannot really occur until the requisite work prior to the action stage takes place (Prochaska et al., 1992). Finally, in the maintenance stage, they are still actively monitoring themselves to assure that the problematic behavior does not resume.

This model assumes that change is not usually linear, but instead is characterized by relapse and occurs gradually. Furthermore, certain processes of change are associated with each stage (Prochaska, Velicer, DiClemente, & Fava, 1988). For example, while precontemplators exhibit little energy to understand their problems, contemplators may benefit from consciousness raising, dramatic relief and self-reevaluation (Prochaska et al., 1988). Individuals in preparation begin to take small steps toward action and use counter-conditioning and stimulus control. Those in the action stage emphasize behavioral processes (e.g., stimulus control and counter-conditioning) over experiential processes (Prochaska et al., 1988). Individuals in a maintenance stage continue to use behavioral strategies as long as their commitment to change is supported by a valued sense of self and the support of another person. A prospective study conducted by Perz, DiClemente, and Carbonari (1996) showed that engaging in experiential process activities during contemplation and preparation stages and shifting to behavioral process activities when in action predicted successful stage transition.

Transtheoretical Model As Applied to Batterers

Recently, the TTM has been used to conceptualize the process of violence cessation among domestic abusers (Begun, Shelley, & Strodthoff, 2002; Brownlee, Ginter, & Tranter, 1998; Daniels & Murphy, 1997; Levesque, Gelles, & Velicer, 2000). Investigators have begun to develop assessment instruments specifically designed to measure readiness to change among domestic violence offenders. For example, exploratory principal components analysis on a sample of 1,359 batterers and confirmatory factor analysis with additional samples have demonstrated that the 35-item Safe at Home assessment is comprised of three scales consistent with the precontemplation, contemplation and preparation/action stages outlines in the transtheoretical model (Begun, Murphy, Bolt, Weinstein, Strodthoff, Short, & Shelley, 2003). Concurrent validity was suggested by evidence that low readiness to change in the Safe at Home measure was correlated with little assumption of personal responsibility for violence and with minimization of psychological aggression, contemplation scores were negatively associated with minimization of own aggression (as assessed by comparison with partner reports), and preparation/action scores were significantly correlated with self-efficacy for abstaining from verbal aggression. Levesque et al. (2000) developed a measure of domestic violent offender readiness to change, based on items similar to those in the University of Rhode Island Change Assessment (URICA) model. They provided evidence of concurrent validity with self-reported strategies to end the violence, self-reported use of psychological aggression, degree of partner blame and decisional balance. However, they did not compare responses to partner report. The

URICA-DV was also not successful in predicting attrition in a sample of 302 French-speaking males (Brodeau, Rondeau, & Brochu, 2005). Scott (2004) found that attrition was not predicted by batterers' self-report on the original version of the URICA, but was predicted by counselors' ratings of the men's stage of change. Scott and Wolfe (2003), on the other hand, found that the URICA did predict men's outcome in a batterer treatment program, with precontemplators (who comprised 41% of the sample) showing less positive change in empathy, communication and abusive behavior as compared to men in the contemplation and action stages. Alexander and Morris (in press) found that two clusters ("earlier stage of change" and "later stage of change") responding to a DV-relevant version of the original URICA scale differed in their self-report of anger and violence perpetrated, degree of disparity from their partners' report of violence, and response to treatment. Thus, it appears possible to empirically identify those individuals who are in an earlier stage of change and who are significantly less likely to benefit from standard abuser intervention programs.

How to engage these precontemplators in treatment remains a challenge. Daniels and Murphy (1997) noted that interventions for men in precontemplation need to focus on the goals of increasing awareness of the negative aspects of the problem, acknowledging the problem and accurately evaluating oneself. A meaningful focus on the problem is more likely to occur when the client is able to find reasons to change that will meet his own needs, rather than to simply avoid punishment. Thus, motivational discussions such as those developed by Miller and Rollnick (2002) for engaging substance abusers are particularly germane to batterers in this stage. According to Miller and Rollnick (2002), Motivational Interviewing is successful to the extent that it creates a discrepancy or cognitive dissonance within the client as to the target behavior (such as DV) and other desired goals (such as seeing himself as manly or having a wife who cares about him). The best way to achieve this dissonance is to help the client articulate his ambivalence without directly attempting to persuade him (Rollnick & Miller, 1995). As such, the therapist needs to use reflective listening, expression of acceptance, affirmation of the client's freedom of choice and self-direction, and attention to the client's readiness to change. Evidence with substance abusers suggests that motivational techniques are particularly effective among the least motivated clients (Handmaker, 1993; Rollnick, Heather, & Bell, 1992) and those at the greatest risk for relapse (Handmaker, Miller, & Manicke, 1999). Therefore, techniques that focus on enhancing motivation and encouraging contemplation of the DV for one's own personal reasons are particularly appropriate for individuals in the precontemplation stage (Daniels & Murphy, 1997). These strategies are the least likely to be found in standard batterer treatment programs, even though precontemplators comprise a significant proportion of abusers referred for treatment.

Daniels and Murphy (1997) also describe interventions most appropriate for individuals in the contemplation stage, including consciousness raising (e.g., education about the consequences of DV), dramatic relief (e.g., encouraging the expression of feelings about one's past or current problems, an activity obviously requiring the context of a trusting and supportive therapeutic setting), self-reevaluation, and environmental reevaluation (e.g., discovering how the DV affects others and oneself). In addition, contemplation requires a consideration of the costs and benefits of both abusive behavior and of change. Conversely, the preparation and action stages include interventions more typical of standard batterer intervention programs, such as counter-conditioning, stimulus control and contingency management. Daniels and Murphy (1997) emphasize the danger of using preparation and action interventions prematurely; for example, they point out that requiring a no-violence contract before an individual has made a personal commitment to change trivializes its meaning and loses the benefit of its impact at the point at which it would be meaningful to the client. Similarly, Begun et al. (2002) note that the use of action techniques for individuals either in precontemplation or contemplation is ineffective and could inadvertently lead to "pseudosuccess" indicators as opposed to meaningful internalized change. Therefore, attention to the order and timing of interventions is essential.

An on-site pilot group testing these principles with 12 court-ordered offenders showed promising results, exhibiting high levels of cohesiveness, with clients demonstrating progressive willingness to take personal responsibility for their behavior and their role in the relationship problems that led to their referral (Alexander, Morris, Sullivan, & Knutson, 2003). Consistent with the model, clients frequently expressed their desire, commitment or intention to change their maladaptive patterns of relating, and spontaneously requested action-oriented information and assistance, including self-control strategies and communication skills.

In conclusion, the emphasis on behavioral interventions and external change processes found in the Duluth model and standard cognitive-behavioral treatments appears to be inappropriate for the majority of batterers in treatment who are in the precontemplation and contemplation stages of change. Therefore, a format of treatment with greater emphasis on internal change processes (such as suggested by the motivational literature) was expected to be more relevant to and more effective with the preponderance of batterers in treatment.

Individual Readiness to Change as a Potential Moderator of Change

Ideally, a stages of change (SOC) treatment approach would suggest that exercises and interventions be geared to the particular readiness to change of each individual within the group (whether group members are selected for a similar stage of change or whether interventions vary for different individuals within a particular group). Although it is premature to suggest that individual differences in readiness to change can be easily addressed within a given group, it is important to assess each individual's response to treatment within a given group as a function of his readiness to change. For example, it is possible that a SOC approach front-loaded with interventions geared to the precontemplator and early contemplator, while effective for these individuals, would be less effective for the individual in the action stage. In other words, the readiness to change of the individual could be hypothesized to moderate the effectiveness of the proposed treatment format. The implication of such a finding, of course, would be to compose groups of individuals who are relatively homogeneous with respect to their readiness for change and then expose them to a treatment geared to their stage of change.

Working Alliance and Group Cohesion as Indicators of Treatment Effectiveness

Internal change processes may be more effective for precontemplators and contemplators in treatment to the degree that these change mechanisms help to establish a personal connection between the client and the therapist or among group members. This personal connection may help maintain someone's involvement in the treatment until other change mechanisms have begun to have an effect and may also increase the influence of the therapist and the other group members on the individual batterer. Thus, therapeutic alliance (or working alliance) and group cohesion may serve as mediators of treatment effectiveness. Working alliance is defined as the quality of the collaborative relationship between therapist and client, their affective bond, and their ability to agree on treatment goals and tasks (Bordin, 1979; Horvath & Symonds, 1991).

The results of a meta-analysis with psychotherapy clients indicated a moderate, consistent relationship between the therapeutic alliance and outcome (Martin, Garske, & Davis, 2000). Working alliance has been found to predict treatment completion in a battering population (Rondeau, Brodeur, Brochu, & Lemire, 2001) as well as a reduction in psychological and physical aggression at follow-up (Taft, Murphy, King, Musser, & DeDeyn, 2003). In fact, Taft et al. (2003) found that therapists' ratings of working alliance were the strongest predictors of outcome. Moreover, Taft, Murphy, Musser, and Remington (2004) found that readiness to change predicted working alliance, as did lower levels of psychopathy and borderline traits, self-referred status, marital status and higher age and income.

Group cohesion is one of the more important curative factors in group therapy (Yalom, 1985, 1995), predicting improvement and treatment completion (Budman & Soldz, 1993; Lieberman, Yalom, & Miles, 1983; Tschuschke & Dies, 1994). Although Schwartz and Waldo (1999) found that cohesion predicted the number of group meetings attended by batterers, they did not examine whether group cohesion predicted cessation of violence. Conversely, Taft et al. (2003) did find that group cohesion predicted decreased levels of psychological and physical aggression at follow-up. Therefore, both working alliance and group cohesion would appear to be important potential mediators of change in a study of treatment.

Therapist Adherence.
Testing the efficacy of any treatment presupposes that therapists are using interventions prescribed by the approach and are avoiding the use of interventions proscribed by that approach (Waltz, Addis, Koerner, & Jacobson, 1993). Therapist adherence is important not only for the initial training and ongoing supervision of therapists, but also to assess the effect of fidelity to the described treatments. Therapist adherence has been found to predict improved outcome in a variety of treatment modalities (Bright, Baker, & Neimeyer, 1999; Henggeler, Melton, Brondino, Scherer, & Hanley, 1997; Messer & Holland, 1998). In this study, therapist adherence was assessed as an indicator of treatment integrity.

Domestic Violence Among Latinos
Higher rates of DV among minority ethnic groups have been consistently observed (Caetano, Schafer, & Cunradi, 2001; Kessler, Molnar, Feurer, & Appelbaum, 2001), with a greater risk of injury from DV in Hispanics than non-Hispanics (Duncan, Stayton, & Hall, 1999). Moreover, the lower rate of partner concordance about the occurrence of DV within Hispanic than non-Hispanic couples (Caetano, Schafer, Field, & Nelson, 2002) suggests an even higher prevalence of precontemplation within this group. While predictors of attrition from batterer intervention programs have been identified for English-speaking Latinos, these predictors have not been identified for Spanish-speaking Latinos (Hudak, 2001). Therefore, this project presents an opportunity to explore whether a treatment specifically designed for individuals in an earlier stage of change would be particularly relevant for this important but understudied group of batterers.

In conclusion, given the limited effectiveness of existing treatments to successfully engage the majority of batterers (who tend to be in precontemplation and contemplation), the purpose of this study was to develop and test the effectiveness of a group intervention specifically aimed at these batterers. The SOC model has been shown to be relevant to court-ordered batterers (Alexander & Morris, in press; Begun et al., 2003; Daniels & Murphy, 1997;

Eckhardt et al., 2004; Levesque et al., 2000; Scott, 2004; Scott & Wolfe, 2003). Therefore, the development and evaluation of a treatment protocol based on a model with proven effectiveness in engaging another group of individuals also frequently marked by their denial and minimization (i.e., substance abusers) appeared to be warranted. Outcomes included self-report at post-treatment and partner report at follow-up and the potential mediators of attendance, working alliance and group cohesion. Given that the SOC model focuses on individual differences, it was important to assess for the effect of an interaction between an individual's readiness to change and the treatment protocol on outcomes. Although different patterns of outcomes were not anticipated in Spanish-speaking samples, all analyses included this variable. Finally, it was considered essential to assess treatment integrity. A description of the two treatment protocols is included under Methodology. Following a description of data analyses that were conducted, results, discussion of these results and implications for practice will be described.

Methodology

Sampling Plan. The APP's Abuser Intervention Program receives court-referred offenders primarily as a condition of a criminal sentence for a partner abuse charge or as a part of a civil order for protection against domestic violence. APP court-referred participants are 97% male. The significant majority of these male clients (98%) are served in group counseling formats, 80% in the standard 26-week group discussed here and the remainder in a briefer group format. Approximately 20 English-speaking 26-week groups are conducted each year at two locations within Montgomery County. Clients are normally excluded from group treatment if they are actively psychotic, have personality disorders severe enough to disrupt a group, or have very poor ability to communicate in English. Approximately 6-9 Spanish-speaking 26-week groups are also conducted at the APP every year. Clients who are actively abusing alcohol or other drugs are enrolled in substance abuse programs and are required to have one month of sobriety before they are eligible to begin group treatment.

Male clients who were referred to the Montgomery County APP and who were appropriate for participation in either the English-speaking or Spanish-speaking 26-week group were randomly assigned to one of the group treatment conditions as described below. Except for the Group Cohesion Scale, all batterer self-report and partner data analyzed in this study were already collected routinely by the APP as part of its normal intake and follow-up procedures. All identifying information regarding the batterer and his partner was deleted before any information was sent to the P.I. This proposal was evaluated and approved by the University of Pennsylvania Institutional Review Board.

Establishment of a Safety Plan for Victim Partners.
Victim partners were already routinely contacted and followed by the APP for information regarding the batterer's behavior. The woman was informed that her participation and responses to all questions and questionnaires would remain confidential, within the limits defined by the law. The current project asked no more information of victims than what they were already asked at intake and at follow-up by the APP. As is consistent with the normal operating procedures of the APP, detailed safety plans were made with the woman, and she was given support by agency interviewers, encouraged to seek counseling if distressed and provided with information about shelter services, counseling services, crisis intervention and a 24-hour helpline. Both initial and

follow-up interviews were conducted at a time when she was alone or could obtain privacy. Before conducting phone interviews, interviewers routinely asked the partner whether she had privacy to speak and whether she felt comfortable answering questions. If the woman made it clear that she no longer wished to be contacted by the APP, the agency immediately complied with her request. Finally, in order for a woman's anonymous data to be used as part of this study, she was asked to give her verbal assent.

Data Collection Procedures and Measures

All participants at the APP routinely undergo a standard intake procedure. Data collection consists of 1) an intake interview and questionnaires completed by the batterer at intake, 2) an initial telephone interview of the partner, 3) data collected from the batterer at mid-treatment and post-treatment, 4) data at the end of treatment on the number of sessions attended, and 5) telephone-based follow-up information received from the partner at six and twelve months post-intake. As these data are obtained on all program participants at the APP, they were stripped of all identifying information but were linked to the treatment condition to which the man was randomly assigned and transmitted to the P.I. Data collected from initial and follow-up interviews of partners were similarly removed of all identifying information by APP staff other than an identification number allowing these data to be merged with that collected from the respective batterers. Agency staff also transmitted data obtained at 8 and 16 weeks into the group as well as data regarding the number of sessions attended. The link between the identification number and the batterer's and partner's identity was available only to APP staff and was not available to the P. I.

Abuser Intake Interview. The abuser was asked information regarding his age, education, employment status, income, relationship to the victim partner, current contact, children in common, and history of abuse and trauma. As part of this intake, the offender completed the following instruments which were relevant to the specific hypotheses tested in this study: *The Conflict Tactics Scales-Revised* (CTS2; Straus, Hamby, Boney-McCoy, & Sugarman, 1996) contains an 8-item Psychological Aggression subscale, a 12-item Physical Assault subscale, and a 6-item Injury subscale. The CTS2 Sexual Coercion scale in its entirety was not used because Latina women in particular have previously expressed discomfort with completing items from this scale. Participants responded with respect to the most recent six months and the entire history of the relationship at baseline assessment. Good internal consistency and construct and discriminant validity exist for all subscales (Straus et al., 1996). *The University of Rhode Island Change Assessment* (URICA; McConnaughy, DiCLemente, Prochaska, & Velicer, 1989) is a 32-item scale with subscales for Precontemplation, Contemplation, Action and Maintenance. For use in this study, individuals were instructed to complete the questions with respect to their violence against their intimate partner. Internal consistency (alpha) is good for all scales. *The Personality Assessment Inventory* (PAI; Morey, 1991) Infrequency and Positive Impression Management validity subscales and the Borderline Features and Antisocial Features subscales were used. Internal consistency alphas and test-retest reliability coefficients range from .84 to .91 for the two clinical scales and they correlate significantly with other clinical and personality disorder scales (Morey, 1991). *The Alcohol Use Disorders Identification Test* (AUDIT; Saunders, Aasland, Babor, De La Fuente, & Grant, 1993) is a 10-item screening tool; the cutoff score of 8 has been found to accurately discriminate casual drinkers from problem drinkers (Saunders et al., 1993). Additional items ask about the abuse of drugs. *Generality of Violence-Revised* (GVQ-R). Based on a modification of Holtzworth-Munroe et al.'s (2000) procedure to assess generality of violence, men were presented with a list of 11 violent behaviors from the CTS2 as well as eight categories of people/situations. The frequency of engaging in these behaviors toward each of the people in the categories were then summed, excluding violence against ex-wives/ex-girlfriends (since it constituted intimate violence) as well as violence that was part of a job requirement (e.g., military or police action). *Perceptions of Procedural Justice.* Based on the work on procedural justice by Paternoster et al. (1997), a four-item measure of procedural justice by the criminal justice system was created. It consisted of these items: "Do you believe that the judge listened to your side of the story?", "Do you think that the judge used accurate information in deciding your case?", "Did the judge treat you with dignity and respect?", and "Were you treated by the judge in a way in which most people in your situation would have been treated?" Each item was answered on a four-point scale, ranging from 9 (not at all) to 1 (somewhat) to 2(mostly) to 3 (very much). *The Dissociative Violence Scale* (DVS; Murphy, 2001) contains nine items that inquire about dissociative experiernces during the perpetration of violence, aside from any alcohol or drug-related experiences. The DVS was modeled after a dissociative violence interview used in a prior investigation (Simoneti, Scott, & Murphy, 2000), in which dissociative experiences during violent episodes were found to correlate positively with the frequency and severity of the violence, history of witnessed and experienced abuse in childhood, and both interview and self-report measures of general dissociative symptoms.

Victim Partner Intake Interview. The victim partner was asked about demographics as well as relationship status, children in common, and current contact with the batterer. As part of this interview, the victim partner also completed the following instruments: *The CTS2* items as they pertain to the batterer's behavior toward her in the previous six months and over the course of their relationship (i.e., lifetime). *The Danger Assessment Scale* (DAS; Campbell, 1986, 1995) used by the APP is a 12-item version of Campbell's (1986, 1995; Stuart & Campbell, 1989) DV risk assessment measure (Goodman, Dutton, & Bennett, 2000). Test-retest reliability ranges from .89 to .94 and Cronbach's alpha from .60 to .86 (Campbell, 1995). The DAS has been found to significantly predict re-abuse over a three-month period (Goodman et al., 2000). *The Process of Change in Abused Women Scale.* (PROCAWS; Brown, 1998). Validated on a group of 300 battered women, the PROCAWS 25-ITEM Problems in Relationships Scale asks the respondent of her attitudes toward her partner and the abuse she experienced and assesses her intentions with respect to remaining in the relationship. It loads onto five factors, labeled precontemplation, contemplation, letting go of the hope he'll change (equated by Brown with the preparation stage), action, and autonomy/separate self (equated by Brown with the maintenance stage). For the purposes of this study, only the precontemplation scale was used as a measure of the woman's minimization of the impact of the violence upon her life.

Measures Collected During the Course of Group Treatment. At 8 and 16 weeks into treatment, APP staff administered the following instruments (although data collection of these measures ended up being quite variable). *The Working Alliance Inventory - Short Form* (WAI-S; Tracey & Kokotovic, 1989) has 12 items and assesses a general overriding alliance dimension. Derived by factor analysis from the WAI, it has good concurrent and predictive validity (Horvath & Greenberg, 1986). The WAI-S has good internal consistency for both client and counselor ratings (Tracey & Kokotovic, 1989). Each client completed the WAI-S with reference to the two group therapists overall. Each group co-therapist completed the WAI-S with reference to each group member, with the two therapists' ratings of each client then averaged. *The Group Cohesion Scale* (GES-COH; Moos, 1994) is an 18-item scale consisting of two nine-item subscales measuring the degree of self-reported cohesiveness within a defined group as pertaining to emotional cohesion and task cohesion within the group. The scale's reliability and validity are good (Moos, 1994) and its predictive validity of outcome has been demonstrated in studies of therapy groups, including groups of sexual offenders (Beech & Fordham, 1997) and aggressive inpatients (Lanza, Satz, Stone, Kayne, et al., 1995).

Description of Treatment Formats

Stage of Change Treatment Format. An outline of the protocol for the SOC treatment is found in Table 1. Although not an integral aspect of the TTM, an SOC treatment format relies upon a Motivational Interviewing (MI) perspective to define the therapist's stance (Velasquez et al., 2001). MI is relevant to all stages of change but is especially suited to dealing with individuals in an earlier stage of change (Miller & Rollnick, 2002). Therapists conducting groups in the SOC condition were trained and supervised extensively in an MI approach. Important facets of an MI approach include asking open-ended questions, asking about both positive and negative aspects of the problem, listening reflectively with attention to guessing verbally as to the meaning and emotions behind a client's statements, being willing to revise these reflections upon clarification from the client, affirming the client's efforts to change, and summarizing to prepare the client to move on and to reflect his ambivalence around a given issue (Miller & Rollnick, 2002). Consistent with this approach, emphasis was placed on nurturing the group as a whole and on facilitating the establishment of norms (e.g., acceptance of others, maintaining confidentiality, development of group cohesiveness, willingness to self-disclose and to accept feedback, mutual respect, and an emphasis on the "here and now") known to be curative effects in groups (Yalom, 1995).

As can be seen in Table 1, the first several sessions in the SOC group format consisted of an introduction to the stages of change as they relate to DV. The first 14 sessions relied upon the change processes known to be particularly useful for individuals in the precontemplation and contemplation stages. The final 12 sessions focused on processes of change more characteristic of individuals in the preparation, action and maintenance stages (including specific behavioral techniques such as stimulus control, counter conditioning, reinforcement management, self-efficacy, self-liberation, and the use of helping relationships to maintain one's change in behavior). Shortly after the onset of this study, a decision was made to move the session on values and goals to Week 3. Therapists and supervisors concluded that this was an important strategy for referring back to discrepancies between one's stated values and one's behavior throughout the course of the group.

Cognitive-Behavioral Gender-Reeducation Format. An outline for the protocol for the CBTGR treatment is found in Table 2. This standard abuser intervention program focuses on the risk of continued abuse by participants and attempts to quickly give the clients tools they can use in their everyday lives. Thus, it uses behavioral techniques from the very beginning of the group (e.g., time out strategies, anger journal). Also, because of its roots in the feminist perspective, it immediately addresses the minimization and denial that surround DV by working to have clients directly acknowledge their use of abuse in the first session and to engage in a meaningful discussion of pros and cons of abuse by the second session. The exercises and homework assignments that were used in this format are for the most part well-known and have been used in many North American batterer intervention programs. As noted before, the order of assignments was inconsistent with a SOC model and the general stance of the group leaders toward the group members was confrontational towards clients' minimization, denial and justification of their abuse.

Training of Group Leaders. Group leaders employed by the APP are masters-level mental health professionals with the senior group leaders normally having at least two years full-time experience working with abusers (and possibly, victims). Separate pairs of group leaders conducted the SOC groups and the CBTGR groups to avoid the danger of confounding of the two treatment conditions. Group leaders in each condition received approximately eight hours of training in their respective treatment formats prior to the onset of this study. In addition, group leaders were supervised bi-weekly with respect to their assigned treatment formats, during which attention was given to their adherence to their assigned treatment condition.

Modeling of Underlying Stage of Change.

As noted by Scott and Wolfe (2003), several researchers who have used the TTM to guide the development of interventions with other populations have questioned whether the stages are truly distinct or instead comprise a continuum (cf., Sutton, 2001; Weinstein, Rothman & Sutton, 1998). This distinction would not affect treatment in that either scenario would imply the need for different types of interventions for individuals at either different stages or different points on this dimension. Nonetheless, as will be described below, an examination of the URICA data indicated the appropriateness of viewing these data as reflective of a continuous dimension, as opposed to a set of discrete stages.

The URICAs collected from a sample of 1,554 men in treatment for domestic violence (in conjunction with Grant R49/CCR321284-01 funded by the Centers for Disease Control) provided the basis for testing whether the four subscales of the URICA could be modeled as a continuous underlying model of change. The Mplus structural equation modeling software was used for this analysis. First, confirmatory factor analysis was performed on the four subscales designed to assess increasingly advanced stages of change. These factor models showed that the items within each subscale generally had good reliability estimates. The second stage was to model variation in distinct patterns of scores on the URICA subscales consistent with the Stage of Change model. This was accomplished using latent variable mixture modeling to evaluate and compare alternative solutions. A solution reflecting progression in the stage of change process was selected. The final step involved predicting the position of individuals along an underlying continuous-level latent change process variable, using both estimated class membership probabilities and item response theory-based mapping of class membership on the continuous change process. Men's post-treatment responses on the URICA were then compared to their position on the initial continuous-level variable, in order to assess their movement from intake to post-treatment with respect to their underlying stage of change. Their initial underlying stage of change was also used in subsequent analyses assessing the interaction of stage of change with treatment condition in predicting outcomes, as will be described below. (A more complete description of this analysis can be provided upon request.)

Specific Hypotheses

1. It was hypothesized that participation in the SOC treatment format would result in significant change relative to participation in the CBTGR condition, including:

a) greater desistance from violence (as assessed by self-report scores of violent behavior at post-treatment and partners' report of violent behavior and psychological abuse at follow-up);

b) greater assumption of responsibility for one's violent behavior over the course of treatment (as assessed by a greater degree of change on the URICA from pre-treatment to post-treatment).

II. It was hypothesized that the changes described above would be mediated by greater involvement in the treatment program, as assessed by:

a) decreased attrition (i.e., a greater number of sessions attended);

b) higher working alliance (as assessed by clients and therapists);

c) higher group cohesion (as assessed by clients).

III. It was hypothesized that the SOC treatment condition would be particularly effective for men in an earlier stage of change as reflected by an interaction between treatment condition and a continuous measure of initial stage of change on desistance from violence.

IV. It was hypothesized that participants in the Spanish-speaking SOC treatment condition would tend to show the same benefits as those of the English-speaking participants (namely, greater desistance from violence, greater assumption of responsibility for their violent behavior, and greater involvement in the treatment program). In other words, cultural background was not expected to moderate the effect of treatment condition, although this variable was included in all analyses.

V. It was hypothesized that blind ratings of audiotapes of treatment sessions would significantly differentiate the behavior of counselors in the two treatment conditions.

Results.

Sample
The sample consisted of 528 batterers, 96.1% of whom were court-ordered to treatment. (The APP does not differentially assign men to groups based on whether they are court-ordered or self-referred.)

Random Assignment of Men to Groups. Men were randomly assigned to one of the two group conditions, although with some limits. For example, while groups in both conditions were regularly scheduled on Monday through Thursday evenings (with a recent addition of Saturdays), insofar as possible, men were only assigned to groups on days that their work schedule permitted and as soon as a new group in either condition was available. Moreover, in order to assure maximal adherence to a particular group condition, therapists only led groups in one condition. This affected assignment to a group to the extent that a new group in a particular condition could only be started when therapists for that condition became available (as a function of completing other groups). While this only minimally affected assignment to English-speaking groups (given that more English-speaking therapists were available), this did affect assignment to Spanish-speaking groups in that the therapists conducting the CBTGR groups happened to have more time available to run groups than did the therapists conducting the SOC groups. As a consequence, a total of 19 English-speaking groups were conducted in the SOC condition (with a total of 200 men), 16 English-speaking groups in the CBTGR condition (with a total of 175 men), 4 Spanish-speaking groups in the SOC condition (with a total of 47 men) and 10 Spanish-speaking groups in the CBTGR condition (with a total of 106 men). The following analyses describe the composition of men in these group conditions. Comparisons were made to assess the comparability of men in the two different treatment conditions across two different languages spoken.

Demographics. Overall, men in this program were an average of 35.1 years old (SD = 9.7) and had an average of 11.5 years of education (SD = 4.5). With respect to ethnicity, 21.6% of the men described themselves as White/Caucasian, 32.5% were Black/African-American, 36.3% were Latino, 3.2% were Asian-American, 0.8% were Native American, and 5.6% were of another ethnicity. With respect to immigration status, 40% of the men in these groups were immigrants with most from Latin America (23.9%), 6.1% from Africa, 3.3% from the Caribbean and the rest from other areas of the world. They represented 73 different countries of origin.

Information on their partners was less complete in that only 157 partners were successfully contacted at intake. Overall, victim partners were an average of 32.8 years old (SD = 9.2) with an average of 12.5 years of education (SD = 3.3). With respect to ethnicity, 27.2% of the women described themselves as White/Caucasian, 28.2% were Black/African-American, 36.9% were Latina, 4.1% were Asian-American, 0.3% were Native American, and 3.3% were of another ethnicity. With respect to marital status, 31.2% of the couples were married but separated, 30.8% were married and currently living together, 23% were never married, 7.3% were not married but currently living together, 5.9% were divorced and 1.8% were widowed. With respect to immigration status, 25.7% of the women described themselves as immigrants, although information on this variable was frequently missing. With respect to current relationship status, 45.3% of the couples described themselves as currently in a relationship with each other. With respect to children, 22.2% had children, with varying custody arrangements.

Although it was possible to have had several simultaneous sources of referral, the overall breakdown of referral source was as follows: 55.5% criminal court referral (including supervised parole, unsupervised parole, probation before judgment, prosecution diversion and prerelease), 35.6% civil order of protection, 2.2% juvenile court referral (including juvenile court order and child welfare plan), 2.8% pretrial referral, and 3.9% self-referred. For purposes of further analyses, these categories were collapsed into court-mandated (96.1%) and self-referred (3.9%). Overall, 10.5% of the men in this study had been admitted multiple times. Multiple admissions either reflected having been admitted to the APP on multiple occasions or reflected a man's lack of compliance with a group leading to his having been discharged from a group and subsequently transferred to another group. (Being transferred from one group to another because of scheduling problems occurred only rarely and was not considered a "multiple admission.")

In determining the comparability of men assigned to groups, comparisons were made first between English- and Spanish-speaking men, and then within English-speakers and within Spanish-speakers, between men assigned to the two treatment conditions. As can be seen in Table 3, men assigned to English-speaking and Spanish-speaking groups differed in a number of ways. For example, Spanish-speakers were younger, less educated, less likely to be employed, more likely to be Latino, and more likely to be an immigrant. Partners of Spanish-speakers were similarly younger and less educated. Although Spanish-speaking couples were more likely to have children, they did not differ from English-speaking couples either with respect to their relationship status (whether or not they were currently in a relationship with each other) or their marital status. English- and Spanish-speaking men also did not differ with respect to their specific source of referral, their general source of referral (court-mandated vs self-referred) or whether they had multiple admissions.

Insert Table 3 about here.

When English-speakers were compared with respect to demographic characteristics as a function of their assignment to the two group conditions, they did not differ with respect to age, partner age, education, partner education, employment status, number of children, marital status, ethnicity, source of referral (either specifically or court-mandate/self-referral), or multiple admissions. Similarly, Spanish-speakers did not differ as a function of treatment type with respect to age, partner age, education, partner education, employment status, number of children, marital status or ethnicity. While Spanish-speakers in the two group conditions did not differ with respect to specific referral source or multiple admissions, men in the SOC condition were somewhat less likely to have been court-mandated and somewhat more likely to have been self-referred. Overall, however, men in the two treatment conditions were comparable with respect to demographics.

Lifetime Intimate Partner Violence. Both the men's and their partners' responses to the CTS provided a basis for describing initial levels of lifetime violence for their relationship. As can be seen in Table 4, Spanish-speakers reported having perpetrated significantly less psychological aggression, physical aggression and injury against their partners than did English-speakers. On the other hand, although based on a much smaller number, partners of Spanish-speakers did not differ from partners of English-speakers with respect to the amount of lifetime psychological aggression and physical aggression they reported that they had experienced at the hands of their partner and actually reported having experienced significantly more injury and sexual coercion than did partners of English-speakers. Interestingly, Spanish-speaking men reported that their female partners had perpetrated significantly less psychological aggression and physical aggression against them than did English-speakers, while the female partners of Spanish-speakers themselves reported having perpetrated significantly more psychological aggression and physical aggression than did the female partners of English-speakers.

Insert Table 4 about here.

These apparent discrepancies in reports of lifetime violence were also observed in paired comparison t-tests. While English- and Spanish-speakers did not differ in their agreement with their partners about past psychological aggression, Spanish-speakers were much more likely to be discrepant from their partners with respect to lifetime physical aggression (p = .03), lifetime injury (p = .006), lifetime sexual coercion (p < .001), lifetime psychological aggression by the female partner (p = .027), and lifetime physical aggression by the female partner (p < .001). Thus, consistent with other literature on domestic violence among Latino couples, there appears to be significantly less consensus among Latino couples than among Anglo couples (Caetano et al., 2002). On the other hand, female partners of English-speakers and Spanish-speakers did not report any difference with respect to their perceptions of the dangerousness of the men on the DAS.

Neither English-speakers nor Spanish-speakers differed on either their self-reported or partner-reported lifetime perpetration of psychological aggression, physical aggression or injury or their level of dangerousness on the DAS as a function of their assignment to either a CBTGR or SOC condition. Therefore, men in the two treatment conditions did not differ initially on their level of violence severity (based either on their self-report or partner-report) or perceived dangerousness.

Psychopathology and Trauma History. Overall, only 3% of men exceeded clinical cutoff scores for antisocial traits on the PAI and only 9.3% exceeded clinical cutoff scores for borderline traits, although these scores may have been affected in part by invalid responses. As can be seen in Table 5, English- and Spanish-speaking men were found to differ significantly on two validity measures on the PAI; Spanish-speakers exhibited more social desirability ("positive impression management") and more infrequent responses. Therefore, comparisons were conducted covarying for these two validity measures. Results of ANCOVAs indicated that Spanish-speakers scored significantly higher on a measure of antisocial behavior. The two groups did not differ on the PAI measures of borderline traits and suicidality or on the AUDIT measure of alcohol abuse, but Spanish-speakers reported significantly less drug use than did English-speakers. Neither English-speakers nor Spanish-speakers differed with respect to borderline traits, suicidal tendencies or alcohol or drug abuse as a function of their assignment to the two treatment conditions, but Spanish-speakers in the SOC condition did score significantly higher on the measure of antisocial behavior than did the Spanish-speakers in the CBTGR condition.

Insert Table 5 about here.

Overall, 30.5% of men reported a childhood history of physical abuse, 35.2% reported a history of verbal abuse, 14% reported a history of sexual abuse, and 18.9% reported having witnessed violence between their parents in childhood. With respect to partners' report, 27.5% of the women reported a history of physical abuse in childhood, 36.9% reported a history of verbal abuse in childhood, 14.8% reported a history of sexual abuse, 37.8% reported having witnessed violence between their parents in childhood, and 21.9% reported having experienced violence in previous relationships in adulthood. Spanish-speaking men reported having experienced significantly less verbal abuse and less sexual abuse than did English-speaking men, although the partners of English- and Spanish-speakers did not differ with respect to childhood history of family violence or whether or not they had experienced violence in a previous relationship in adulthood. Finally, neither English-speakers nor Spanish-speakers differed with respect to childhood trauma histories on the basis of their assignment to the two treatment conditions, although the partners of English-speaking men in the SOC condition reported a somewhat greater history of having witnessed violence between parents in childhood.

Outcomes

Desistance from Violence as a Function of Treatment

Self-Report. Men completed the CTS questionnaire (as it pertained to the previous six months) at the end of treatment. Therefore, post-treatment data only existed for men who were compliant enough to still be present at the end of treatment. As can be seen in Figures 1 - 2 below, responses to the CTS are low frequency behaviors and the data were greatly skewed, precluding the use of data transformations.

Insert Figures 1 – 2 about here.

Therefore, men's post-treatment behavior was categorized as either acknowledging or denying the use of psychological and physical aggression toward their partner during the preceding six months. Logistic regression analysis was then used to assess the effect of type of treatment and language on these outcomes. As can be seen in Table 6, results suggested that there was no effect of either treatment condition or language spoken on either men's self-reported psychological aggression or physical aggression at post-treatment.

Insert Table 6 about here.

Victim Report at Follow-up. Victim partner follow-up was conducted approximately six and twelve months from the date of intake. A total of 114 victims were contacted at follow-up. However, because of intermittent staffing shortages, seasonal variation in intakes and men either dropping out of groups or being transferred to other groups, there was inevitably variability in the length of time between intake and a man's assignment to a group. For example, some victim follow-ups (N = 22) were considered unusable because they were actually conducted either shortly before or shortly after the partner had been ultimately assigned to a group and therefore could not be used to evaluate the effectiveness of that group. An additional follow-up was considered unusable because the date of the contact was not specified. Some variability also occurred between intake dates and successful attempts to contact victims. Therefore, the decision was made to combine six and twelve-month victim follow-ups, covarying for the length of time between the man's actual startdate for a group and when the victim follow-up was conducted. When both six and twelve-month follow-ups were available for the same victim, the long-term follow-up was used. Follow-up reports from a total of 91 women constituted the basis for the logistic regression analyses described below.

On one hand, as can be seen in Figures 3 - 5 below, means on the CTS scales of Psychological Aggression, Physical Aggression and Injury were consistent in suggesting the relative effectiveness of the SOC condition over the CBTGR condition in reducing these outcomes.

Insert Figures 3 – 5 about here.

However, as can be seen in Figures 6 - 8 below, these CTS data are quite skewed (not unexpectedly, given the low frequency of the behavior), beyond which any data transformation could justifiably be used.

Insert Figures 6 – 8 about here.

Therefore, victims' data were categorized into whether or not psychological aggression, physical aggression and injury had occurred during the previous six months and logistic regression analyses were conducted, covarying for the length of time between the startdate for the group and the follow-up. Importantly, whether or not a partner had been contacted for follow-up did not differ as a function of either treatment type or language spoken.

As can be seen in Table 6 above, results of the logistic regressions suggested that treatment type was not significant in predicting victim report of either psychological aggression or injury at follow-up. However, the overall model was significant in predicting victims' report of physical aggression at follow-up ($X^2 = 11.53$, p = .009). Treatment type was significantly predictive of victim report of physical aggression at follow-up (p = .042) as was the length of time between group startdate and follow-up (p = .025) while language spoken was not. Namely, SOC treatment was associated with significantly less physical aggression at follow-up as was a greater length of follow-up time.

In an attempt to further identify the source of treatment effects for reduced physical aggression, this logistic regression was re-run for English- and Spanish-speakers separately. While not significant for Spanish-speakers, the overall model was significant in predicting victims' report of physical aggression by English-speakers ($X^2 = 10.83$, p = .004). Specifically, the SOC treatment type was associated with victims' decreased likelihood of reporting physical aggression at follow-up (p = .019) and the longer the follow-up time, the less physical aggression experienced by the victim (p = .048).

Finally, paired comparison t-tests were conducted to assess whether there was any change in the amount of psychological and physical aggression and injury victims reported they had experienced in the previous six months from intake to the follow-up report. The greatest reduction was observed in victims' reports of psychological aggression (t = 3.23, df = 32, p = .003), presumably because the range was greater than in either physical aggression (t = 2.22, df = 23, p < .04) or injury (t = 1.92, df = 22, p < .07). However, consistent with results from the logistic regression analyses, change in psychological aggression was not differentially associated with treatment.

Assumption of Responsibility as a Function of Treatment

As described previously, men's movement from intake to post-treatment with respect to their underlying stage of change was modeled with the use of structural equation modeling. Given that the change in URICA was by definition a normally distributed variable, a two-way analysis of variance was used to assess the effect of treatment type and language spoken on

change in URICA. As can be seen in Table 7, results indicated that neither treatment type nor
language spoken nor the interaction of these two variables predicted change in growth from
intake to post-treatment.

Insert Table 7 about here.

A regression analysis was then conducted to assess whether this change could be
predicted by individual or partner characteristics. Individual variables hypothesized to have an
effect on change in URICA included self-reported lifetime psychological and physical
aggression, higher borderline and antisocial personality traits, conditions that could be presumed
to interfere with one's acknowledgement of one's violent behavior (alcohol abuse, drug abuse,
and domestic violence-related dissociation), and one's partner's minimization of the severity of
the abuse (i.e., the partner's degree of precontemplation as assessed by the PROCAWS). Results
of this regression analysis were significant (Adjusted R^2 = .24, F (8, 84) = 4.60, p < .001), with a
lack of acknowledgement of one's lifetime physical aggression towards one's partner at intake
predictive of a greater degree of change in the URICA (t = -4.33, p < .001) and with one's
partner's minimization of the severity of the violence predictive of less change in the URICA (t
= -2.64, p = .01).

Mediators of Change

Attendance. *Effect of Treatment Type.* Men were only considered as having been
assigned to a given group if they attended at least one session. Results of a two-way ANOVA
suggested that Spanish-speakers were significantly more likely overall to attend a greater number
of sessions (p = .005), with Spanish-speakers in the CBTGR condition particularly likely to
attend sessions (p < .04). These findings may reflect in part the commitment of APP's Spanish-
speaking therapists overall and especially in the CBTGR condition to ensure their group
members' compliance (including the use of make-up sessions more than was typical in English-
speaking groups); however, there was no overall effect of treatment condition on the number of
sessions attended.

Treatment Completion. From a statistical perspective, it is always preferable to use the
full range of a variable; thus, the number of sessions attended conveys more information than
does "treatment completion," a variable that is somewhat arbitrary at best anyway (Buttell &
Pike, 2002; Daly et al., 2001; McCloskey et al., 2003). However, in order to allow comparisons
to other treatment studies, comparisons were also conducted on the basis of treatment
completion, defined as attendance of at least 75% or greater. Overall, 21.4% of individuals who
completed at least one session (and therefore were included in this sample) dropped out of
treatment prematurely. The two treatment conditions did not differ in the percentages of their
participants who were considered to have satisfactorily completed treatment as opposed to
dropped out of treatment (X^2 = .98, df = 1; with 53.2% of individuals in the CBTGR and 46.8%
of individuals in the SOC condition completing treatment).

Individual Predictors of Attendance and Treatment Completion. Based on current
research findings on attrition and attendance, demographic variables (age, education,
employment, immigration status), referral source (court-referred vs self-referred), self-identified
problems with violence (self-reported CTS lifetime psychological and physical aggression

scores, and general violence), personality variables (borderline and antisocial traits), and initial
stage of change (level of underlying stage of change at intake) were assessed for their ability to
predict the number of sessions attended. The overall model was modestly significant (Adjusted
$R^2 = .09$, F (11, 222) = 3.00, p = .002). Namely, the number of sessions attended was positively
predicted by employment (t = 3.13, p = .002), by age (t = 2.42, p < .02), and by elevated
borderline traits (t = 2.17, p < .04). This regression equation was then re-run separately for
participants in the CBTGR and SOC treatment conditions. For men in the CBTGR condition,
the model was significant (Adjusted $R^2 = .09$, F (11, 116) = 2.20, p = .019) with employment (t =
3.09, p = .002) and borderline traits (t = 2.22, p < .03) both positively associated with increased
attendance. For men in the SOC condition, the model was also significant (Adjusted $R^2 = .09$, F
(11, 94) = 1.95, p = .043) with age (t = 2.67, p = .009) and having been court-mandated to
treatment (t = 2.38, p = .02) both positively associated with increased attendance. When
conducted on Spanish-speaking men only, this model was not significant (Adjusted $R^2 = .06$, F
(10, 35) = 1.26, *ns*).

A series of MANOVAs was then conducted to assess whether these traits differentiated
treat completion rates between the two conditions. Neither treatment completion nor its
interaction with treatment condition was significantly associated with the demographic variables
of age, education, employment and immigration status. On the other hand, both treatment
completion (F (5, 450) = 2.54, p < .03) and its interaction with treatment condition (F (5, 450) =
2.35, p = .04) were marginally significantly associated with personality and violence
characteristics. Univariate ANOVAs clarified that men who were higher on either antisocial
traits (F (1, 454) = 5.94, p = .015) or general violence (F (1, 454) = 4.88, p < .03) were less likely
to successfully complete treatment if they were enrolled in the SOC condition. Neither treatment
completion nor its interaction with treatment condition was significantly associated with initial
underlying stage of change.

Attendance and Desistance from Violence. In order to assess whether treatment
attendance (i.e., number of sessions attended) was related to a man's desistance from violence, a
series of ANOVAs was conducted comparing the number of sessions attended by partners of
women who had or had not reported psychological aggression, physical aggression and injury at
follow-up. Given that some victim follow-ups were conducted before the group had actually
ended, it was necessary to limit follow-ups to those women who were contacted at least six
months after the group startdate. Although the number of sessions attended was unrelated to
whether or not a victim reported having experienced psychological aggression at follow-up, the
partners of those victims who reported having experienced physical aggression at follow-up (F
(1, 53) = 6.81, p = .012) attended significantly fewer sessions. (There were not enough
incidences of injury reported at follow-up to assess the relationship between treatment
attendance and the perpetration of injury.) Similarly, results of a chi square analysis suggested
that partners of men who completed treatment were significantly less likely to have experienced
physical aggression at follow-up than were partners of men who did not complete treatment (X^2
= 6.47, df = 1, p = .011). Therefore, a lack of compliance with treatment was an indicator of
increased or continued risk to one's partner at follow-up.

Working Alliance. In order to test the hypothesis that working alliance would be
enhanced by participation in the SOC condition, two-way analyses of variance were conducted
on the therapists' assessment of working alliance at 8 weeks (averaged across the reports of the

two therapists with respect to each group member), therapists' assessment of working alliance at 16 weeks, clients' assessment of working alliance at 8 weeks, and clients' assessment of working alliance at 16 weeks. Therapists in the Spanish groups reported significantly higher levels of working alliance at 16 weeks ($F (1, 133) = 35.68$, $p < .001$) than did therapists in the English groups. There was no main effect of treatment type, but there was a significant interaction between language and treatment type ($F (1, 133) = 15.85$, $p < .001$), suggesting that the therapists in the CBTGR condition were even more likely to report good working alliance with group members. With respect to client report of working alliance, clients at 16 weeks in the Spanish groups also described significantly higher levels of working alliance across both treatment types ($F (1, 127) = 28.34$, $p < .001$). There was also some evidence of correlation between therapists' and clients' assessment of working alliance at both 8 weeks ($r = .32$, $p = .014$) and at 16 weeks ($r = .22$, $p = .018$). Therapists' assessment of working alliance at 16 weeks was positively correlated with the total number of sessions attended ($r = .24$, $p = .005$), suggesting either that their assessment of working alliance was affected by men's attendance or that their assessment of a positive working alliance actually facilitated men's attendance. However, there was no other indication that either therapists' or clients' assessment of working alliance at either 8 or 16 weeks was predictive of men's self-reported change on the CTS subscales or URICA or victims' report of aggression at follow-up.

Insert Table 8 about here.

Group Cohesion. Two-way ANOVAs were also conducted on clients' assessment of the emotional aspects of group cohesion at 8 and 16 weeks and clients' assessment of the task aspects of group cohesion at 8 and 16 weeks. At 8 weeks, neither the emotional nor the task aspects of group cohesion were significantly related to treatment type, language spoken or the interaction between these two factors. On the other hand, at 16 weeks, there was a significant main effect of language spoken on the emotional aspect of group cohesion ($F (1, 85) = 4.96$, $p = .029$) and a trend toward significance of language spoke on the task aspect of group cohesion ($F (1, 85) = 3.62$, $p = .061$), such that Spanish groups across both treatment types reported higher levels of group cohesion. Not unexpectedly, clients' assessment of working alliance at 8 weeks was significantly correlated with their assessment of both emotional group cohesion ($r = .29$, $p = .028$) and task group cohesion ($r = .27$, $p = .047$) at 8 weeks, and their assessment of working alliance at 16 weeks was even more correlated with their assessment of emotional group cohesion ($r = .51$, $p < .001$) and task group cohesion ($r = .47$, $p < .001$) at 16 weeks. Group cohesion was not significantly related to the number of sessions attended (unlike the findings of Schwartz & Waldo, 1999), to self-reported change on the CTS scales or the URICA, or to partner follow-up reports of psychological aggression, physical aggression or injury.

Insert Table 9 about here.

Interaction of Treatment and Initial Stage of Change on Desistance from Violence.

In order to assess whether the SOC curriculum was especially effective for individuals in an earlier stage of change, a series of analyses was conducted to assess the effects of an interaction between initial underlying stage of change and treatment format on desistance from violence (based on self-report at post-treatment and partner report at follow-up). First, a series of logistic regression analyses was conducted to assess the effects of language spoken, treatment condition, level of underlying stage of change at intake and the interaction between treatment condition and initial stage of change on self-reported violent behavior at post-treatment. There was no evidence of an interaction between treatment condition and initial stage of change on either self-reported psychological aggression or physical aggression at post-treatment. Second, the effects of these variables (and most importantly, of the interaction between treatment condition and initial underlying stage of change) on victim reports at follow-up were assessed. Results of logistic regression analyses suggested that there was no significant effect of these variables on victim report of psychological aggression or injury at follow-up. On the other hand, there was a significant effect on victim report of physical aggression at follow-up ($X^2 = 21.77$, $p < .001$), such that in addition to an effect of initial underlying stage of change ($p < .04$) and an effect of treatment type ($p < .02$), there was a significant interaction between treatment type and underlying stage of change ($p = .01$). Namely, partners of men who were in an earlier stage of change reported less physical aggression at follow-up when the men were in the SOC condition whereas partners of men who were in a later stage of change reported less physical aggression at follow-up when the men were in the CBTGR condition. Using a median split to illustrate low vs high initial stage of change, an approximation of this relationship is depicted in Figure 9.

Insert Figure 9 about here.

Therapist Adherence

To assure that group therapists were indeed using only those interventions prescribed by their particular treatment approach (Waltz et al., 1993), a rater who was blind to the treatment condition listened to randomly selected audiotapes from each 26-week group for which audiotapes were available. The audiotapes were rated on general but unique counselor behaviors presumed to be associated with the SOC treatment approach (including encouraging reflection, focusing on clients' values and motivations, expressing empathy for clients' experience, using open-ended questions, briefly summarizing clients' responses and exploring further, and making reflective statements) as well as general but unique counselor behaviors presumed to be associated with the CBTGR treatment approach (including adopting the role of the expert, confronting clients about their abusive behavior, presenting reasons why clients should change, appealing to external authority to help clients see why they should change, focusing on client behaviors, and encouraging a change of controlling and abusive behavior). Items were interspersed from both conditions into 12-item scales (six items reflecting the attributes positively associated with the treatment condition and six items reverse-coded to reflect the attributes of the other condition). (See Appendix A.) The items were then rated as to their presence on a scale from 1 to 5. Cronbach's alpha for each of these scales was .889. On the basis of 36 coded audiotapes, the two treatment conditions were significantly differentiated by the ratings on the scales ($F (1, 34) = 7.20$, $p = .011$).

Additional Analyses

Generalizability of Victim Follow-up Findings. In an effort to assess how generalizable these findings were to the whole population, comparisons were made between those men whose partners were successfully contacted for follow-up with those men whose partners were not able to be contacted. (Men had supplied demographic information on their partners when the partners had not been successfully contacted at intake.) With respect to demographics, the men whose partners were contacted were somewhat older (p < .04) as were their partners (p = .002) and reported a longer relationship time (p < .001), although their marital status did not differ from those partners who were not contacted. While partners of immigrants were no more or less likely to be contacted, a higher percentage of women who were themselves immigrants were contacted at follow-up (X^2 = 15.32, p < .001). In general, few differences were found between couples for whom partner follow-up was obtained and those couples for whom it was not. They did not differ in other demographic aspects, such as employment status, ethnicity, language spoken or degree of contact. Importantly, successful follow-up contact with women did not differ as a function of either the man's or the partner's report of his previous lifetime violence toward her, the generality of his violence outside the home, her perception of his dangerousness, or his level of psychopathology. It is not clear whether men whose partners were not contacted were any less likely to benefit from treatment, given that men did not differ on the number of sessions attended or on any self-reported change in violence or URICA as a function of whether or not the partner was contacted. However, based on intake data gathered from both men and women, the absence of any apparent selection biases characterizing women who were contacted for follow-up argues for the generalizability of findings from partner follow-up data.

Effect of Source of Referral. A series of chi-squares was conducted to assess whether men responded differentially to treatment as a function of their source of referral (court-mandated vs self-referral). While there was no effect of treatment type and source of referral on victims' report of either psychological aggression or injury at follow-up, there was a modest indication of differential response to treatment as a function of source of referral with respect to victims' report of physical aggression at follow-up. Namely, follow-up reports did not differentiate men in the CBTGR condition as a function of their source of referral (X^2 = 0.53, df = 1, ns); on the other hand, partners of men in the SOC condition were somewhat less likely to report physical aggression at follow-up if the men were court-mandated to treatment as opposed to self-referred (X^2 = 3.99, df = 1, p < .05). (This finding was based on small numbers and should be viewed cautiously.)

Multiple Admissions. Exploratory ANOVAs and chi-squares were conducted comparing men with multiple admissions to those with only a single admission. Men with multiple admissions were younger (p = .001), described themselves as more generally violent (p < .05), more antisocial (p = .023), more suicidal (p = .03), dissatisfied with the justice system (p = .004), and less likely to be an immigrant (p < .05). They were less likely to be married, whether or not they were currently living with their partner (p < .04). They did not differ from single admissions on their ethnicity or self-report of lifetime violence. Their partners also did not describe them as more violent or more dangerous than did partners of single-admission men; in fact, their partners reported that they were less likely to have been violent with other women (p < .03). Their partners did not differ from other partners in any other way except that they were more likely to report having witnessed domestic violence in childhood (p = .004).

A series of chi-squares was conducted to assess whether men with multiple admissions to groups were any more likely to be described by their partners at follow-up as psychologically aggressive, physically aggressive or injurious. There was no effect of multiple admissions on victims' report of psychological aggression or injury. On the other hand, men with multiple admissions to groups were significantly more likely to be described as physically aggressive at follow-up (X^2 = 7.88, p = .005), in that only 13.2% of men who were on their first admission to a group were categorized as being physically aggressive at follow-up whereas 60% of men who had multiple admissions were categorized as being physically aggressive at follow-up.

Chi-squares were also conducted to assess whether there was any indication of differential treatment effectiveness for men with multiple vs single admissions. (These are exploratory findings because of low numbers.) For first-time offenders (i.e., single admissions), there was no example of injury perpetrated at follow-up by men who were in the SOC condition, whereas 9.6% of partners of men in the CBTGR condition reported having experienced injury at follow-up (X^2 = 3.97, p < .05). There was no differential effect of treatment condition on victims' follow-up reports of psychological or physical aggression. For men with multiple admissions, there was no significant effect of treatment type on victims' report of psychological aggression, physical aggression or injury at follow-up.

Correlates of Trauma History. A man's self-reported trauma history in childhood was associated with an increased self-report of general violent tendencies (child physical abuse with general violence, r = .17, p < .001; and child sexual abuse with general violence, r = .21, p < .001), and with both antisocial and borderline tendencies (child physical abuse with antisocial traits, r = .16, p = .001 and with borderline traits, r = .23, p < .001; child sexual abuse with borderline traits, r = .21, p < .001; child witnessing violence with borderline traits, r = .16, p = .002). Child sexual abuse history was also negatively correlated with the victim's report of injury (r = -.28, p < .04) and sexual coercion (r = -.39, p = .005) at intake, possibly suggesting that simply a man's willingness to acknowledge a history of child sexual abuse may be protective in some ways.

A woman's history of physical abuse was associated with her partner's self-disclosure of greater psychological aggression (r = .34, p < .001) and physical aggression (r = .22, p = .01) at intake, but also with his report of greater psychological aggression (r = .26, p = .002) and physical aggression (r = .19, p = .02) on the part of the woman. A woman's history of child sexual abuse was associated with her partner's admission of physical aggression at intake (r = .21, p < .02). A woman's history of witnessing violence was associated with her partner's admission of psychological aggression (r = .21, p < .02) and physical aggression (r = .21, p < .02) at intake as well as her assessment of his dangerousness at intake (r = .23, p < .02). Her trauma history was not, however, associated with her report of his lifetime violent behavior toward her. Finally, her report of abuse in previous adult relationships was associated with her partner's admission of injury toward her (r = .20, p = .021) and with his report of her psychological aggression toward him (r = .22, p = .009), but not with any report on her part.

Discussion

The purpose of this study was to compare the effectiveness of a new batterer group treatment curriculum, based on the Stages of Change model and Motivational Interviewing, with a standard treatment curriculum, based on cognitive behavioral therapy and Duluth-model premises. As Sartin, Hansen and Huss (2006) have recently noted, while a number of research studies have compared batterer intervention to no treatment, few comparisons have been made of different types of

treatment. One of the main strengths of this study was its use of randomized assignment of men to
groups. The success of randomization was made evident by the lack of differences between men in
the two treatment formats with respect to demographics, source of referral, severity of DV (based on
both self-report and partner-report), generality of violence, psychopathology and trauma history.

Effects of Treatment

The overall goal of any batterer treatment program is desistance from violence. Differences
between the two treatment formats did not emerge with respect to men's self-reports of violence at
the end of treatment. Differences did emerge in partners' reports of physical aggression at follow-
up. Overall, significantly fewer partners of men assigned to the SOC treatment condition as opposed
to the CBTGR condition reported having experienced physical aggression in the previous six
months. The fact that reports of physical aggression decreased as time went on suggests that the
reported changes in behavior were real and not just an artifact of the monitoring of behavior that
occurs during program attendance. Victim follow-up reports are not only considered the gold
standard of evaluation studies of batterer intervention (in that they are a much more conservative
measure of recidivism, Babcock et al., 2004), but in this study they were also obtained on program
drop-outs as well as completers. Therefore, these reports clearly allowed an evaluation of the ability
of the two conditions to both maintain men's involvement in treatment as well as alter their violent
behavior. As will be described further with respect to the limitations of this study, there were a
limited number of partner follow-up reports. Nonetheless, a comparison of men and their partners as
a function of whether or not partner follow-up was obtained suggested that these partner follow-ups
were notably representative of the full sample.

Differences between the two treatment conditions were not observed with respect to partner
follow-up reports of psychological aggression and injury. The lack of differences observed with
respect to reports of injury may have been due in part to a floor effect – i.e., there were very few
instances of injury reported by partners overall at follow-up (N = 5 out of 96 follow-up reports). On
the other hand, the continuing occurrence of psychological aggression is troubling and typical of
batterer treatment outcome studies (Hamberger & Hastings, 1988; Johannson & Tutty, 1998;
Rosenfeld, 1992). Victims' experience of psychological aggression was not eliminated as a function
of their partners' participation in either condition; however, paired comparison t-tests suggest that it
was significantly reduced, albeit not differentially by treatment condition.

Evidence on therapist adherence suggested that counselors were behaving in ways
characteristic of their respective treatment conditions. That is, counselors in the SOC condition
were more likely to encourage reflection, focus on clients' values and motivations, express empathy
for clients' experience, use open-ended questions, briefly summarize clients' responses and explore
further, and make reflective statements. Conversely, counselors in the CBTGR condition were more
likely to adopt the role of the expert, confront clients about their abusive behavior, present reasons
why clients should change, appeal to external authority to help clients see why they should change,
focus on client behaviors, and encourage a change of controlling and abusive behavior. That the
SOC and CBTGR conditions were operating differentially and in ways consistent with their
respective theoretical underpinnings was also suggested by several significant interactions. For
example, there was a significant interaction between initial stage of change and treatment condition
in that men in an earlier stage of change at intake were more likely to benefit from the SOC
condition (as indicated by their partners' reports of physical aggression at follow-up) while men in a
later stage of change at intake were more likely to benefit from the standard CBTGR condition.

Consistent with these findings, exploratory analyses of the effects of source of referral on victim reports of physical aggression at follow-up suggested that men who were court-referred as opposed to self-referred were more likely to benefit from the SOC curriculum whereas there was no differential effect of CBTGR treatment as a function of source of referral.

One final indication that the SOC condition was differentially effective for men in an earlier stage of change emerged from the regression analyses predicting treatment attendance in the two conditions. Consistent with Cadsky et al.'s (1996) notion of the importance of lifestyle instability in predicting treatment compliance, men in both the SOC and CBTGR conditions were more compliant with treatment to the extent that they showed evidence of lifestyle stability (i.e., being employed in the CBTGR condition and being older in the SOC condition). Moreover, other more meaningful differences between the two curricula in the prediction of treatment attendance emerged. Namely, being court-mandated was a significant predictor of the number of sessions attended by men in the SOC condition (consistent with the partner follow-up reports of men who were court-mandated and enrolled in the SOC condition). On the other hand, elevated borderline traits was a significant predictor of treatment compliance in men enrolled in the CBTGR condition, suggesting that this treatment format may be more useful for individuals who are inherently motivated whether because they are in a later stage of change or because their own level of internal distress (as indicated by elevated borderline traits) serves to facilitate their attendance.

Therefore, in spite of its apparent success with most individuals, the SOC treatment condition also had its limitations. It was no more effective than standard treatment in reducing the aggressiveness of men with multiple admissions. Consistent with this finding, it was less effective than the CBTGR condition in retaining men in treatment who had personality disorders (borderline traits associated with the prediction of number of sessions attended and antisocial traits/generally violent behavior associated with the prediction of treatment completion). While treatment retention is certainly a necessary goal of any treatment intervention, it is not necessarily sufficient for good outcomes, especially with personality-disordered individuals who are known to respond more poorly to treatment (Dutton et al., 1997).

At the other end of the spectrum, the SOC condition also was not as effective either for men who initially were in a more advanced underlying stage of change or who were self-referred. It is likely that men who are initially highly motivated for change (including men who are self-referred) are seeking very explicit strategies for controlling their behavior, such as time-out or communication skills. For them, the consciousness-raising that is characteristic of the earlier portion of the SOC curriculum may be frustrating. Possible alternatives for men who are self-referred might include the use of shorter-term groups focusing on specific anger-management and conflict resolution skills. Another suggestion would be for therapists to make greater use of a menu of options, as would be consistent with a Motivational Interviewing approach - in other words, to describe an array of strategies earlier in the curriculum without necessarily promoting those strategies.

Mediators of Change

Exactly why the SOC curriculum was generally more effective was less clear. The two conditions did not differ with respect to any of the proposed indicators of increased involvement (attendance, working alliance or group cohesion). Moreover, although increased attendance was associated with women's decreased report at follow-up of physical aggression, neither working alliance nor group cohesion predicted women's follow-up reports. The validity of men's reports of working alliance was underscored by the observed agreement between group therapists and group members and by correlations between group members' assessment of their working alliance with their perceptions of both emotional and task cohesiveness within the group. Given the findings of other researchers regarding the importance of working alliance in decreasing aggression (Brown & O'Leary, 2000; Taft et al., 2003), this is an important potential mediator of change in batterer treatment. Future research needs to continue to focus more on identifying which aspects of a treatment format are associated with change (Sartin et al., 2006). Therefore, a more extensive evaluation of therapist adherence might also provide information relevant to this question.

Men's Stages of Change

In addition to the interaction between initial stage of change and treatment condition in predicting desistance from violence, there was a small but significant main effect of initial underlying stage of change on victims' report of physical aggression at follow-up. Scott and Wolfe (2003) found that self-reported stage of change based on the original URICA predicted self-reported and partner-reported change in abusive behavior. The current study did not find that initial stage of change predicted self-reported behavior on the CTS at post-treatment, but did find an effect of initial stage of change on partner follow-up report. Initial underlying stage of change did not predict either the number of sessions attended or treatment completion in either condition. This was consistent with the findings of Scott (2004) and Brodeur, Rondeau, and Brochu (2005) and was perhaps due to its negative correlation with the PAI measure of positive impression management ($r = -.28$, $p < .001$). Therefore, although the construct of stage of change is certainly relevant to predicting change over time (as is also indicated by its correlation with victims' follow-up reports), as a self-report measure, it is subject to social desirability.

Based on men's self-reports at the beginning and end of treatment, differential growth in stages of change was not observed between treatment conditions. Instead, men who were less likely to acknowledge their abusive behavior at intake (and who also tended to score higher on the PAI measure of positive impression management) were more likely to show change in their URICA scores at post-treatment. This could either simply reflect a statistical regression to the mean or could indicate that both treatment formats facilitated a decrease in denial and an increase in the assumption of responsibility for abusive behavior, a worthy goal of any batterer intervention program. For example, Brownlee and Chlebovec (2004) found that variations on the common theme of accepting responsibility (including recognition of abusive behaviors and admission of wrongdoing) characterized men's positive evaluations of a treatment program.

Interestingly, men's eventual assumption of responsibility for their behavior was also influenced by the degree to which their partners did or did not minimize the violence at intake. While this should not be surprising, analyses of men's stages of change and even progress in treatment typically fail to recognize the role of the partner's views of the violence, assuming instead that court-mandates and the treatment itself will necessarily have more influence over a man's behavior toward his partner than her own views of the violence. This finding of the apparent relevance of a partner's view of the violence to the man's view of the violence should serve as an important reminder that agencies must intervene with women (at least those who tend to minimize the violence) as well as with men in order to assure a desistance of violence.

Spanish-Speakers' Behavior in Group Treatment

Overall, cultural background (as reflected by the language spoken in the group) did not moderate the effect of treatment on outcomes. This was the case even though some of the observed differences between Spanish-speakers and English-speakers could be presumed to affect their behavior in treatment. The Spanish-speaking men in this sample were generally less educated with a lower standard of living than the English-speakers. They also showed significantly more evidence of denial of their behavior, as seen both by their decreased level of interpartner agreement about their violence and by their elevated scores on the two PAI validity measures used in this study. These findings are consistent with the observations of Caetano et al. (2002) and others who report increased disparity of report in Latino couples. Whether these men's denial was due to a lack of awareness of the cultural unacceptability of violence within this country or to a lack of psychological sophistication, their denial is undoubtedly a challenge in their treatment.

However, in spite of certain characteristics that could impede response to treatment, Spanish-speakers were significantly more compliant with treatment, perhaps in part due to their perception of the potential power of the court-system over their legal immigration status. (In fact, a regression model predicting the number of sessions they attended was not significant, presumably in part due to restricted range in the dependent variable.) Alternatively, their increased compliance could be due to their increased working alliance with their therapists and to their perception of group cohesion. The differential effects of these group dynamics deserve greater attention.

Men with Multiple Admissions

Although they comprised a small percentage (10.5%) of those seen in group treatment at the APP, men with multiple admissions remain a significant challenge for any batterer intervention program. Overall, they were younger and less likely to be married. In other words, they were comparable to Cadsky et al's (1996) description of the batterer with lifestyle instability. Not surprisingly, in this study, they were more dissatisfied with the justice system than were men with single admissions. However, although they scored higher on a measure of antisocial behavior and acknowledged being more generally violent, their partners did not describe them as any more violent or dangerous than did partners of men with single admissions. In fact, partners of men with multiple admissions described them as less likely to have been violent with other women. The fact that these women were more likely to have witnessed domestic violence themselves as young children suggests that they may have been either too inured to the violence or too intimidated to report it accurately at intake.

There was no evidence of differential response to treatment for these men as a function of treatment type; however, both their self-reports and victim follow-up reports suggested that they were at significant risk for ongoing violence. It is clear that the nature of their increased risk must be emphasized to their partners, who may have their own tendency toward minimizing the violence. Moreover, the necessity of a coordinated community response would appear to be especially essential for working with these men (cf., Babcock & Steiner, 1999; Murphy, Musser, & Maton, 1998).

Intervening with Men and Women with a History of Childhood Trauma

As other research has also shown, a history of childhood trauma (whether it be physical abuse, sexual abuse or witnessing violence) increases a man's tendency to be more generally violent and to be characterized by antisocial and borderline traits (Dutton et al., 1997; Holtzworth-Munroe et al., 2000). Even when dealing with the issues of cultural context (e.g., the relative denial of a history of abuse among Spanish-speakers in this study), an effective treatment curriculum needs to address the role of abuse history as an important determinant of affective lability, general aggression, violence-related dissociation, and a distorted view of intimate relationships. In spite of the initial resistance of some group members, most men participating in treatment at the APP found sessions that focused on family history to be cathartic, illuminating and powerful in increasing their sense of cohesiveness and mutual understanding within the group. These sessions were also judged by therapists to be extremely helpful in developing men's sense of empathy toward themselves and their partners.

Some victims of intimate partner violence are at increased risk because of their own history of trauma. For example, in this sample, a woman with a history of witnessing violence between her parents was more likely to be the partner of a man with multiple admissions; she did not describe him as any more violent than did the partners of first-time offenders, even though he himself acknowledged more antisocial traits, generally violent behaviors, and more severe psychologically and physically violent behavior toward her. Moreover, she was also at increased risk of injury at follow-up and was at increased risk of multiple abusive relationships in adulthood. A woman's childhood history of sexual abuse also appeared to be associated with increased risk both at intake and, in the form of self-reported sexual coercion by her partner, at post-treatment. Therefore, it should never be concluded that effective batterer treatment obviates the need for intervening directly with women who are at increased risk because of their own history of trauma. Instead, whether considering both men's and women's history of childhood trauma, a woman's history of previous abusive relationships in adulthood, or the interactive effect of each partner's view of the violence on the other partner's views or behavior, this study clearly points to the necessity of examining DV within the larger context of family violence as a whole (cf., Sartin et al., 2006). Even the impact of treatment on the behavior of men in dual-trauma couples clearly deserves more attention.

Therapists' Reactions to the SOC Curriculum

Therapists at the APP who conducted groups using the SOC curriculum were almost universally enthusiastic about its use. They liked that it was less didactic and that it gave them more latitude in responding to the individual needs of men in the group and to the group overall. They reported encountering much less resistance by group members. At the same time, the decision to move the discussion of values to earlier in the curriculum allowed the therapists to continually highlight men's personal and individualized discrepancies between values and behavior and thus to challenge the men without appearing confrontational. They also reported that group members appeared to respond well to the curriculum. The convergence between therapists' impressions and victims' reports at follow-up of less aggression by men who participated in this curriculum justifies its further development and use, especially for men court-ordered to treatment.

Implications for Future Research

Both the number and follow-up time of partner reports are important characteristics of evaluation studies. With increased numbers of partner follow-ups, it would be possible to assess among other things whether an interaction between men's and women's stages of change predicted outcome. While longer follow-up times in this study were associated with decreases in violence, moderators of this relationship need to be investigated. Similarly, more complete data on therapist adherence would allow an examination of the predictive effects of individual components or attributes of treatment (such as therapist confrontation) on outcomes.

The diversity of batterers seen in this study suggests an opportunity to look at the role of group composition on outcomes. Group therapists and theorists invariably refer to the importance of group composition in its effect on both treatment completion and outcomes (cf., Yalom, 1985, 1995), yet little research has actually looked at its impact on batterer treatment. One exception is a study conducted by Taft et al. (2001) in which racial composition of treatment groups (percentage of African Americans within each group) was examined and found not to predict number of sessions attended for either African Americans or Caucasians. However, other factors such as the percentage of immigrants, the range of age and education of group members, the number of individuals clinically elevated on borderline or antisocial traits and the overall level of stage of change and the impact of these factors on the outcomes of group members, including attendance, working alliance and group cohesion, may yield significant results.

Chang and Saunders' (2002) finding that a batterer's history of childhood trauma led to more attrition from a process-psychodynamic group format that focused more on experiences of child abuse suggests that a more fine-tuned analysis of group dynamics is essential. For example, although most men and therapists in this study were enthusiastic about group sessions that focused on family history, what is the effect of a session on family history on the future short-term or long-term attendance of group members with a history of trauma?

Finally, the significant interaction between treatment condition and an individual's initial underlying stage of change suggests that a treatment format based upon a Stage of Change model necessarily requires an attempt at matching men's stage of change with the appropriate treatment. The logistics of accomplishing this goal can be daunting, especially at smaller agencies with few simultaneous groups. One option would be to adopt a treatment format with different phases (cf., Gerlock, 2001) characterized by interventions appropriate for men in either an earlier or later stage of change. Scott's (2004) evidence of the validity of therapists' ratings of men's stage of change suggests that such a strategy could be clinically feasible. Alternatively, there may be benefits of having a range of stages of change within any group in that it allows precontemplators to be confronted by others (personal communication with Jean Lauderback, February 5, 2007). In any case, this issue of client/treatment matching deserves further attention.

Limitations of Study

In spite of very promising results, this study needs to be viewed within the context of its limitations. First, the number of partner follow-ups obtained was low at less than 25%. There are several reasons for this, including the reliance upon clinical staff to make the initial partner contacts and the lack of compensation for female partners. Both the use of research staff to contact partners and the compensation of partners are essential in achieving a satisfactory partner contact rate (personal communication with Ed Gondolf, December 22, 2005). On one hand, the lack of any noticeable differences between women who were and women who were not contacted for follow-up argues for the validity of the findings. On the other hand, the limited numbers of follow-up reports precluded the exploration of more complicated interactions between treatment and other conditions that would contribute to a more nuanced evaluation of the use of the SOC curriculum. Second, supervision of the CBTGR condition was more sporadic than that of the SOC condition, due to the ongoing health problems of the supervisor of that condition as well as the transition to a new supervisor. In addition, while group therapists were generally compliant with expectations about supervision, there was certainly variability of their attendance in both treatment conditions. Overall, APP therapists tend to be highly experienced and have been using their standard CBTGR curriculum for some time, suggesting that its use was a good representation of the CBTGR curriculum as it is practiced in most venues. Third, the relatively low number of group therapists who regularly audiotaped their sessions (and the technical problems of others who did) precluded an analysis of the differential impact of therapist adherence on the effectiveness of any particular group. In any case, the training of group therapists and the overall adherence of therapists to their respective curriculum suggests that therapists were using the exercises prescribed for that particular treatment model and generally engaging in counseling behaviors prescribed by the respective treatment condition. Finally, there was significant variability in therapists' allegiance to standard APP policies, including the allowance of unexcused absences or the provision of make-up sessions. Some men who were noncompliant were sent back to court while others were assigned to a new group. Moreover, in a venue as big as Montgomery County, Maryland, there was variability in the response of the court when someone was not compliant with treatment.

However, many of the limitations described above actually argue for the significance of outcomes found in this study. Men were randomly assigned to whatever new group was available in conjunction with their schedule. Comparisons of men and their partners across treatment conditions with respect to demographics, lifetime violence, psychopathology, multiple admissions, trauma history and source of referral showed that this imperfect but real-life strategy of random assignment was indeed effective in producing groups that were essentially identical. Differences in outcomes could thus be reliably attributed to differences in the treatment conditions.

Group therapists were generally cooperative with project expectations but the variability of their conscientiousness (for example, in audiotaping sessions, attending supervision sessions, administering measures of group dynamics, complying with standard agency policies) is also a realistic factor confronting any agency that provides services. Therefore, this project shares many of the benefits of both highly-controlled efficacy studies and real-life evaluations of treatment effectiveness (cf., Seligman, 1995). As Henggeler (2004) has argued with respect to a different treatment format, ongoing evaluations of the SOC treatment approach as it is used in actual agencies with ongoing monitoring of therapist adherence and further consideration n of its strengths and limitations are essential in order to judge its effectiveness and provide a basis for its modification and further development.

References

Alexander, P. C., & Morris, E. (in press). Stages of change in domestic violence and the response to treatment. *Violence and Victims.*

Alexander, P. C., Morris, E., Sullivan, R., & Knutson, S. (2003). Stages of change group treatment approach for batterers: A pilot study. Unpublished manuscript.

Augusta-Scott, T., & Dankwort, J. (2002). Partner abuse group intervention: Lessons from education and narrative therapy approaches. *Journal of Interpersonal Violence, 17,* 783-805.

Babcock, J. C., Green, C. E., & Robie, C. (2004). Does batterers' treatment work?: A meta-analytic review of domestic violence treatment outcome research. *Clinical Psychology Review, 23,* 1023-1053.

Babcock, J. C., & Steiner, R. (1999). The relationship between treatment, incarceration, and recidivism of battering: A program evaluation of Seattle's coordinated community response to domestic violence. *Journal of Family Psychology, 13,* 46-59.

Beech, A., & Fordham, A. S. (1997). Therapeutic climate of sexual offender treatment programs. *Sexual Abuse: Journal of Research and Treatment, 9,* 219-237.

Begun, A. L., Murphy, C., Bolt, D., Weinstein, B., Strodthoff, T., Short, L. & Shelley, G. (2003). Characteristics of the Safe at Home instrument for assessing readiness to change intimate partner violence. *Journal of Social Work Research, 13,* 80-107.

Begun, A. L., Shelley, G., & Strodthoff, T. (2002). Adapting a stages of change approach in intervention with individuals who are violent with their intimate partners. *Journal of Aggression, Maltreatment & Trauma, 5,* 105-127.

Bordin, E. S. (1979). The generalizability of the psychoanalytic concept of the working alliance. *Psychotherapy, 16,* 252-260.

Brannen, S. J., & Rubin, A. (1996). Comparing the effectiveness of gender-specific and couples groups in a court-mandated spouse abuse treatment program. *Research on Social Work Practice, 6,* 405-424.

Bright, J. I., Baker, K. D., & Neimeyer, R. A. (1999). Professional and paraprofessional group treatments for depression: A comparison of cognitive-behavioral and mutual support interventions. *Journal of Consulting & Clinical Psychology, 67,* 491-501.

Brodeur, N., Rondeau, G., & Brochu, S. (2005, July). Using the transtheoretical model to predict attrition among men in domestic violence intervention programs. Paper presented at the 9th International Family violence Research Conference, Portsmouth, NH.

Brown, J. (1998, July). *The Process of Change in Abused Women Scales (PROCAWS).* Paper presented at the Program Evaluation and Family Violence Research Conference, Durham, NH.

Brown, P. D., & O'Leary, K. D. (2000). Therapeutic alliance: Predicting continuance and success in group treatment for spouse abuse. *Journal of Consulting and Clinical Psychology, 68,* 340-345.

Brownlee, K., Ginter, C., & Tranter, D. (1998). Narrative intervention with men who batter: An appraisal and extension of the Jenkins model. *Family Therapy, 25,* 85-96.

Budman, S. H., Soldz, S., Demby, A., Davis, M., et al. (1993). What is cohesiveness? An empirical examination. *Small Group Research, 24,*199-216.

Buttell, F. P., & Pike, C. K. (2002). Investigating predictors of treatment attrition among court-ordered batterers. *Journal of Social Service Research, 28,* 53 – 68.

Cadsky, O., Hanson, R. K., Crawford, M. & Lalonde, C. (1996). Attrition from a male batterer treatment program: Client-treatment congruence and lifestyle instability. *Violence and Victims, 11,* 51-64.

Caetano, R., Schafer, J., & Cunradi, C. B. (2001). Alcohol-related intimate partner violence among White, Black, and Hispanic couples in the United States. *Alcohol Research & Health, 25*, 58-65.

Caetano, R., Schafer, J., Field, C., & Nelson, S. M. (2002). Agreements on reports of intimate partner violence among White, Black and Hispanic couples in the United States. *Journal of Interpersonal Violence, 17*, 1308-1322.

Campbell, J. C. (1986). Assessment of risk of homicide for battered women. *Advances in Nursing Science, 8*, 36-51.

Campbell, J. C. (1995). Prediction of homicide of and by battered women. In J. C. Campbell (Ed.), *Assessing dangerousness: Violence by sexual offenders, batterers, and child abusers* (pp. 96-113). Thousand Oaks, CA: Sage.

Cattaneo, L. B., & Goodman, L. A. (2003). Victim-reported risk factors for continued abusive behavior: Assessment the dangerousness of arrested batterers. *Journal of Community Psychology, 31*, 349-369.

Chang, H. & Saunders, D. G. (2002). Predictors of attrition in two types of group programs for men who batter. *Journal of Family Violence, 17*, 273 – 292.

Daly, J. E., & Pelowski, S. (2000). Predictors of dropout among men who batter: A review of studies with implications for research and practice. *Violence and Victims, 15*, 137-160.

Daly, J. E., Power, T. G., & Gondolf, E. W. (2001). Predictors of batterer program attendance. *Journal of Interpersonal Violence, 16*, 971-991.

Daniels, J. W., & Murphy, C. M. (1997). Stages and process of change in batterers' treatment. *Cognitive and Behavioral Practice, 4*, 123-145.

Davis, R. C., & Taylor, B. G. (1998). Does batterer treatment reduce violence? A synthesis of the literature. Report to the U. S. Department of Justice.

Davis, R. C., & Taylor, B. G. (1997). A proactive response to family violence: The results of a randomized experiment. *Criminology, 35*, 307-333.

Davis, R. C., Taylor, B. G., & Maxwell, C. D. (1998). Does batterer treatment reduce violence? A randomized experiment in Brooklyn. *Justice Quarterly, 18*, 171-201.

Duncan, M. M., Stayton, C. D., & Hall, C. B. (1999). Police reports on domestic incidents involving intimate partners: Injuries and medical help-seeking. *Women & Health, 30*, 1-13.

Dunford, F. W. (1998, July). *Experimental design and program evaluation.* Paper presented at the International Family Violence Research Conference, Durham, NH.

Dunford, F. W. (2000). The San Diego Navy experiment: An assessment of interventions for men who assault their wives. *Journal of Consulting and Clinical Psychology, 68*, 468-476.

Dutton, D. G., & Corvo, K. (2006). Transforming a flawed policy: A call to revive psychology and science in domestic violence research and practice. *Aggression and Violent Behavior, 11*, 457-483.

Dutton, D. G., Bodnarchuk, M., Kropp, R., Hart, S. D., & Ogloff, J. P. (1997). Client personality disorders affecting wife assault post-treatment recidivism. *Violence and Victims, 12*, 37-50.

Eckhardt, C. I., Babcock J. C., & Homack, S. (2004). Partner assaultive men and the stages and process of change. *Journal of Family Violence, 19*, 81-93.

Edleson, J. L., & Syers, M. (1990). Relative effectiveness of group treatments for men who batter. *Social Work Research and Abstracts, 26*, 10-17.

Feder, L., & Forde, D. (1999, July). A test of the efficacy of court-mandated counseling for convicted misdemeanor domestic violence offenders: Results from the Broward Experiment. Paper presented at the International Family Violence Research Conference, Durham, NH.

Ford, D. A., & Regoli, M. J. (1993). The criminal prosecution of wife batterers: Process, problems, and effects. In N. Z. Hilton (Ed.), *Legal responses to wife assault* (pp. 127-164). Newbury Park, CA: Sage.

Gerlock, A. A. (2001). A profile of who completes and who drops out of domestic violence rehabilitation. *Issues in Mental Health Nursing, 22,* 379-400.

Gondolf, E. (1997a). A comparison of four batterer intervention systems: Do court referral, program length, and services matter? *Journal of Interpersonal Violence, 14,* 41-61.

Gondolf, E. W. (1997b). Batterer programs: What we know and need to know. *Journal of Interpersonal Violence, 12,* 83-98.

Gondolf, E. W. (2001). Limitations of experimental evaluation of batterer programs. *Trauma, Violence, & Abuse, 2,* 79-88.

Gondolf, E. W. (2004). Evaluating batterer counseling programs: A difficult task showing some effects and implications. *Aggression and Violent Behavior, 9,* 605-631.

Goodman, L. A., Dutton, M. A., & Bennett, L. (2000). Predicting repeat abuse among arrested batterers: Use of the Danger Assessment Scale in the criminal justice system. *Journal of Interpersonal Violence, 15,* 63-74.

Grann, M., & Wedin, I. (2002). Risk factors for recidivism among spousal assault and spousal homicide offenders. *Psychology, Crime & Law, 8,* 5-23.

Gurman, A. S., & Kniskern, D. P. (1978). Deterioration in marital and family therapy: Empirical, clinical, and conceptual issues. *Family Process, 17,* 3-20.

Hamberger, L. K., & Hastings, J. E. (1988). Skills training for treatment of spouse abusers: An outcome study. *Journal of Family Violence, 3,* 121-130.

Handmaker, N. S. (1993). Motivating pregnant drinkers to abstain: prevention in prenatal care clinics. Unpublished doctoral dissertation, University of New Mexico.

Handmaker, N. S., Miller, W. R., & Manicke, M. (1999). Findings of a pilot study of motivational interviewing with pregnant drinkers. *Journal of Studies on Alcohol, 60,* 285-287.

Healey, K., Smith, C., & O'Sullivan, C. (1998). Batterer intervention: Program approaches and criminal justice strategies. Report to the U. S. Department of Justice.

Heckert, D. A., & Gondolf, E. W. (2004). Battered women's perceptions of risk versus risk factors and instruments in predicting repeat reassault. *Journal of Interpersonal Violence, 19,* 778-800.

Hendricks, B., Werner, T., Shipway, L., & Turinetti, G. J. (2006). Recidivism among spousal abusers: Predictions and program evaluation. *Journal of Interpersonal Violence, 21,* 703-716.

Henggeler, S. W. (2004). Decreasing effect sizes for effectiveness studies – Implications for the transport of evidence-based treatments. *Journal of Family Psychology, 18,* 420-423.

Henggeler, S. W., Melton, G. B., Brondino, M. J., Scherer, D. G., & Hanley, J. H. (1997). Multisystemic therapy with violent and chronic juvenile offenders and their families: The role of treatment fidelity in successful dissemination. *Journal of Consulting & Clinical Psychology, 65,* 821-833.

Hilton, N. Z., & Harris, G. T. (2005). Predicting wife assault: A critical review and implications for policy and practice. *Trauma, Violence, & Abuse, 6,* 3-23.

Holtzworth-Munroe, A., Meehan, J. C., Herron, K., Rehman, U., & Stuart, G. L. (2000). Testing the Holtzworth-Munroe and Stuart batterer typology. *Journal of Consulting and Clinical Psychology, 68,* 1000-1019.

Horvath, A. O., & Greenberg, L. S. (1989). The development and validation of the Working Alliance Inventory. *Journal of Counseling Psychology, 36,* 223-233.

Horvath, A. O., & Symonds, B. D. (1991). Relation between working alliance and outcome in psychotherapy: A meta-analysis. *Journal of Counseling Psychology, 38*, 139-149.

Hudak, K. V. B. (2001). An investigation of variables related to attrition of Hispanic men from a domestic violence treatment program. *Dissertation Abstracts International: Section B: The Sciences & Engineering, 61 (11-B),* 6137.

Johannson, M. A., & tutty, L. M. (1998). An evaluation of after-treatment couples' groups for wife abuse. *Family Relations, 47*, 27-35.

Kaplan, R. E. (1982). The dynamics of injury in encounter groups: Power, splitting, and the mismanagement of resistance. *International Journal of Group Psychotherapy, 32*, 163-187.

Kessler, R. C., Molnar, B. E., Feurer, I. D., & Appelbaum, M. (2001). Patterns and mental health predictors of domestic violence in the United States: Results from the National Comorbidity Survey. *International Journal of Law & Psychiatry, 24*, 487-508.

Kingsnorth, R. (2006). Intimate partner violence: Predictors of recidivism in a sample of arrestees. *Violence Against Women, 12*, 917-935.

Lambert, M. J., & Bergin, A. E. (1994). The effectiveness of psychotherapy. In A. E. Bergin & S. L. Garfield (Eds.), *Handbook of psychotherapy and behavior change* (4th ed., pp. 143-189). New York: John Wiley.

Lanza, M. L., Satz, H., Stone, J., Kayne, H. L., et al. (1995). Assessing the impact of group treatment for aggressive inpatients. *Group, 19*, 195-219.

Levesque, D. A., Gelles, R. J., & Velicer, W. F. (2000). Development and validation of a stages of change measure for men in batterer treatment. *Cognitive Therapy and Research, 24*, 175-199.

Lieberman, M. A., Yalom, I. D. & Miles, M. D. (1973). *Encounter groups: First facts.* New York: Basic Books.

Malloy, K. A., McCloskey, K. A., & Monford, T. M. (1999). A group treatment program for male batterers. In L. VandeCreek & T. L. Jackson (Eds.), *Innovations in clinical practice: A source book, Vol. 17.* (pp. 377-395. Sarasota, FL: Professional Resource Press/Professional Resource Exchange, Inc.

Martin, D. J., Garske, J. P., & Davis, M. K. (2000). Relation of the therapeutic alliance with outcome and other variables: A meta-analytic review. *Journal of Consulting and Clinical Psychology, 68*, 438-450.

McCloskey, K. A., Sitaker, M., Grigsby, N., & Malloy, K. A. (2003). Characteristics of male batterers in treatment: An example of a localized program evaluation concerning attrition. *Journal of Aggression, Maltreatment & Trauma, 8*, 67 – 95.

McConnaughy, E. A., DiClemente, C. C., Prochaska, J. O., & Velicer, W. F. (1989). Stages of change in psychotherapy: A follow-up report. *Psychotherapy, 26*, 494-503.

Messer, S. B., & Holland, S. J. (1998). Therapist interventions and patient progress in brief psychodynamic therapy: Single-case design. In *Empirical studies of the therapeutic hour,* pp.229-257. Washington, DC, US: American Psychological Association, 1998

Miller, W. R. (1985). Motivation for treatment: A review with special emphasis on alcoholism. *Psychological Bulletin, 98*, 84-107.

Miller, W. R., & Rollnick, S. (2002). *Motivational interviewing: Preparing people for change. 2nd Edition.* New York: Guilford.

Moos, R. (1994). *The social climate scales: A user's guide.* Palo Alto, CA: Consulting Psychologists Press.

Morey, L. C. (1991). *Personality Assessment Inventory: Professional manual.* Lutz, FL: Psychological Assessment Resources, Inc.

Murphy, C. M., & Baxter, V. A., (1997). Motivating batterers to change in the treatment context. *Journal of Interpersonal Violence, 12*, 607-619.

Murphy, C. M., Morrel, T. M., Elliott, J. D., & Neavins, T. M. (2003). A prognostic indicator scale for the treatment of partner abuse perpetrators. *Journal of Interpersonal Violence, 18*, 1087-1105.

Murphy, C. M., Musser, P. H., & Maton, K. I. (1998). Coordinated community intervention for domestic abusers: Intervention system involvement and criminal recidivism. *Journal of Family Violence, 13*, 263-284.

Palmer, S. E., Brown, R. A., & Barrera, M. E. (1992). Group treatment program for abusive husbands: Long term evaluation. *American Journal of Orthopsychiatry, 62*, 276-283.

Paternoster, R., Bachman, R., Brame, R., & Sherman, L. W. (1997). Do fair procedures matter? The effect of procedural justice on spouse assault. *Law and Society Review, 31*, 163-204.

Pence, E., & Paymar, M. (1993). *Education groups for men who batter: The Duluth model.* New York: Springer.

Perz, C. A., DiClemente, C.C., & Carbonari, J.P. (1996). Doing the right thing at the right time? The interaction of stages and processes of change in successful smoking cessation. *Health Psychology, 15*, 462-468.

Prochaska, J. O., & DiClemente, C. C. (1984). *The transtheoretical approach: Crossing the traditional boundaries of therapy.* Homewood, IL: Dow Jones Irwin.

Prochaska, J. O., DiClemente, C. C., & Norcross, J. C. (1992). In search of how people change: Applications to addictive behaviors. *American Psychologist, 47*, 1102-1114.

Prochaska, J. O., Velicer, W. F., DiClemente, C. C., & Fava, J. (1988). Measuring processes of change: Applications to the cessation of smoking. *Journal of Consulting & Clinical Psychology, 56*, 520-528.

Rollnick, S., & Miller, W. R. (1995). What is motivational interviewing? *Behavioural and Cognitive Psychotherapy, 23*, 325-334.

Rollnick, S., Heather, N., & Bell, A. (1992). Negotiating behaviour change in medical settings: The development of brief motivational interviewing. *Journal of Mental Health, 1*, 252-37.

Rondeau, G., Brodeur, N., Brochu, S., Lemire, G. (2001). Dropout and completion of treatment among spouse abusers. *Violence & Victims, 16*, 127-143.

Rooney, J., & Hanson, R. K. (2001). Predicting attrition from treatment programs for abusive men. *Journal of Family Violence, 16*, 131-149.

Rosenfeld, B. D. (1992). Court-ordered treatment of spouse abuse. *Clinical Psychology Review, 12*, 205-226.

Saunders, D. G. (1996). Feminist-cognitive-behavioral and process-psychodynamic treatments for men who batter: Interaction of abuser traits and treatment models. *Violence and Victims, 11*, 37-50.

Saunders, J. B., Aasland, O. G., Babor, T. F., DeLaFuente, J. R., & Grant, M. (1993). Development of the Alcohol Use Disorders Identification Test (AUDIT): WHO Collaborative Project on Early Detection of Persons with Harmful Alcohol Consumption – II. *Addiction, 88*, 791-804.

Scalia, J. (1994). Psychoanalytic insights and the prevention of pseudosuccess in the cognitive-behavioral treatment of batterers. *Journal of Interpersonal Violence, 9*, 548-555.

Scott, K. L. (2004). Stage of change as a predictor of attrition among men in a batterer treatment program. *Journal of Family Violence, 19*, 37 – 47.

Scott, K. L., & Wolfe, D. A. (2003). Readiness to change as a predictor of outcome in batterer treatment. *Journal of Consulting and Clinical Psychology, 71*, 879-889.

Schwartz, J. P., & Waldo, M. (1999). Therapeutic factors in spouse-abuse group treatment. *Journal for Specialists in Group Work, 24,* 197-207.

Seligman, M. E. P. (1995). The effectiveness of psychotherapy: The Consumer Reports study. *American Psychologist, 50,* 965-974.

Simoneti, S., Scott, E. C., & Murphy, C. M. (2000). Dissociative experiences in partner assaultive men. *Journal of Interpersonal Violence, 15,* 1262-1283.

Stalans, L. J., Yarnold, P. R., Seng, M., Olson, D. E. & Repp, M. (2004). Identifying three types of violent offenders and predicting violent recidivism while on probation: A classification tree analysis. *Law and Human Behavior, 28,* 253-271.

Straus, M. A., Hamby, S. L., Boney-McCoy, S., & Sugarman, D. B. (1996). The revised Conflict Tactics Scales (CTS-2). *Journal of Family Issues, 7,* 283-316.

Stuart, E. P., & Campbell, J. C. (1989). Assessment of patterns of dangerousness with battered women. *Issues in Mental Health Nursing, 10,* 245-260.

Sutton, S. (2001). Back to the drawing board? A review of applications of the transtheoretical model to substance use. *Addiction, 96,* 175-196.

Taft, C. T., Murphy, C. M., Elliott, J. D., & Keaser, M. C. (2001). Race and demographic factors in treatment attendance for domestically abusive men. *Journal of Family Violence, 16,* 385 – 400.

Taft, C. T., Murphy, C. M., King, D. W., Musser, P. H., & DeDeyn, J. M. (2003). Process and treatment adherence factors in group cognitive-behavioral therapy for partner violent men. *Journal of consulting and Clinical Psychology, 71,* 812-820.

Taft, C. T., Murphy, C. M., Musser, P. H., & Remington, N. A. (2004). Personality, interpersonal, and motivational predictors of the working alliance in group cognitive-behavioral therapy for partner violent men. *Journal of Consulting and Clinical Psychology, 72,* 349-354.

Tracey, T. J., & Kokotovic, A. M. (1989). Factor structure of the Working Alliance Inventory. *Psychological Assessment, 1,* 207-210.

Tschuschke, V., & Dies, R. R. (1994). Intensive analysis of therapeutic factors and outcome in long-term inpatient groups. *International Journal of Group Psychotherapy, 44,* 185-208.

Tutty, L. M., Bidgood, B. A., Rothery, M. A., & Bidgood, P. (2001). An evaluation of men's batterer treatment groups. *Research on Social Work Practice, 11,* 645-670.

Velasquez, M. M., Maurer, G. G., Crouch, C., & DiClemente, C. C. (2001). *Group treatment for substance abuse: A stages-of-change therapy manual.* New York, NY: Guilford Press.

Waltz, J., Addis, M. E., Koerner, K., & Jacobson, N. S. (1993). Testing the integrity of a psychotherapy protocol: Assessment of adherence and competence. *Journal of Consulting and Clinical Psychology, 61,* 620-630.

Weinstein, N. D., Rothman, A. J., & Sutton, S. R. (1998). Stage theories and health behavior: Conceptual and methodological issues. *Health Psychology, 17,* 290-299.

Yalom, I. D. (1985). *The theory and practice of group psychotherapy (3rd ed.).* New York: Basic Books.

Yalom, I. D. (1995). *The theory and practice of group psychotherapy (4th ed.).* New York: Basic Books.

Table 1. Montgomery County APP Abuser Intervention Program Stages of Change/Transtheoretical Model Version Session Outline

Session Title	MI/ Change Process
Precontemplation:	
1. ORIENTATION AND INTRODUCTION Introduction to Program Philosophy and Purpose. Review of group contract. Discussion and development of group ground rules, including respect, equality, non-violence, personal awareness and responsibility.	Empathy Evocation Consciousness-Raising
2. DEFINITION OF ABUSE AND STAGES OF CHANGE. Development of a group working definition of abusive behavior. Fredrickson & Babcock Exercises #1 & #2.	Evocation Consciousness-Raising Self-Reevaluation
3. VALUES AND GOALS. Self-assessment exercises and group discussion targeted at clarifying participant values and goals for partner/ family relationships and identifying discrepancies between values and behavior.	Consciousness-Raising Evocation Self Reevaluation
4. CYCLE OF VIOLENCE. Discussion of film *Deck the Halls*. Presentation of concept and implications of progressive nature of cycle. Opportunity for self-assessment and self-reflection.	Evocation Consciousness-Raising Dramatic Relief
5. RECOGNIZING ABUSE/TYPES OF ABUSE. Instruction, group brainstorming and discussion regarding types of abuse and the socio-cultural contexts in which abuse arises. Homework regarding definition and experience of abuse.	Evocation Automony Consciousness-Raising Self-Reevaluation)
6. EFFECTS OF ABUSE ON CHILDREN. Viewing of video *The Children Are Watching*, followed by brainstorming, and small group and board exercise to develop topic. Self-assessment exercise and group discussion to personalize effects.	Empathic evocation Consciousness Raising Self-Reevaluation Dramatic Relief
7. EFFECTS OF ABUSE ON SELF AND PARTNER. Viewing of two short video clips, followed by brainstorming, self-assessment exercises and group discussion to personalize effects.	Empathic evocation Consciousness Raising Self-Reevaluation Dramatic Relief
8. EVALUATING FEEDBACK FROM OTHERS. Group discussion and exercises aimed at helping clients to even-handedly inventory and assess the feedback (positive and negative) about their interpersonal conduct from family/friends/community.	Autonomy Developing Discrepancy Self-Reevaluation Dramatic Relief
Contemplation:	
9. CULTURAL CONTEXT/GENDER ROLES. View *Men's Work* video to facilitate group discussion of inherited gender roles and explore socio-cultural context in which domestic violence occurs.	Consciousness-Raising Evocation Self-Reevaluation

10-11. FAMILY HISTORY. Use of individual genograms and group discussion to explore formative experiences of gender roles, conflict resolution, addictions and mental illness, witnessing partner violence or experiencing child abuse.	Empathic Evocation Dramatic Relief Consciousness-Raising Self Reevaluation
12. BUTTONS. Introduction to concept. Reframing of "buttons" as triggers for both positive and negative experience. Self-assessment and group discussion to explore individual triggers leading to loss of control, potential causes, and alternative solutions.	Consciousness-Raising Evocation Self-Revaluation
13. PROS AND CONS: Introduction to concept of violence as a "decision." Examination of costs and payoffs in light of values and goals articulated in Session 3. Consideration of alternatives and resources for change. Group discussion of potential value of making a written commitment to non-violence via a no-violence contract as a means of vitiating goals.	Consciousness-Raising Decisional Balance Evocation Collaboration Self-Efficacy Social Liberation
Preparation for Change:	
14. PERSONAL RELATIONSHIP/ SAFETY PLAN. Discussion of personal relationship/ safety plan as a means for achieving life and relationship goals articulated by clients in session 3. Provision of no-violence contract for clients who wish to use this as a tool for achieving their goals and values.	Decisional Balance Self-Efficacy Self-Liberation
Action:	
15. ANGER AWARENESS AND TIME OUT. Discussion of, and introduction to, anger awareness and time out procedure as a means of enhancing self-control and the probability of goal/values achievement.	Self-Efficacy Stimulus Control
16. AWARENESS WHEEL/SELF-TALK/SELF-ANGERING THOUGHTS. Instruction and group discussion to further increase overall self-awareness, with particular emphasis on the impact of self-talk and self-angering thoughts on affect and capacity to self-regulate.	Self-Efficacy Collaboration Stimulus Control Counter-Conditioning Reinforcement Management
17. COMBATING SELF-ANGERING THOUGHTS. Group experiments and discussion to explore emotional impact of positive self-talk. Exercises and discussion to enhance ability to substitute positive self-talk for self-angering thoughts.	Self-Efficacy Stimulus Control Counter-Conditioning Reinforcement Management
18. STRESS MANAGEMENT. Instruction and group discussion of self-care and stress management techniques as a means of enhancing self-regulation and goal achievement. Discussion of substance abuse as ineffective method of stress management. Distribution of health and relaxation aids.	Consciousness-Raising Self-Efficacy Collaboration Counter-Conditioning
19-21. COMMUNICATION SKILLS—SPEAKING AND LISTENING. Instruction and group discussion of concept as means of promoting interpersonal effectiveness and goal attainment. Small/large group practice of reflective listening and assertive communication.	Collaboration Self-efficacy Counter-Conditioning Reinforcement Management
22. CONFLICT RESOLUTION. Didactic and dyadic/small/large group practice of 6 Step Program for Resolving Conflict.	Counter-Conditioning Reinforcement Management

23. TWO KEYS: INTERDEPENDENCE AND EMPATHY. Discussion of romantic notions of partner relationships and relational poles of enmeshment and interdependence, as well as pros and cons of each pole, with aim of developing realistic and individually workable relationship expectations. Exercise in applied perspective taking, leading to reflection of partner's experience of client's past behavior and self-reevaluation by client of any changes indicated in view of insights gained.	Collaboration Decisional Balance Self-Liberation Stimulus Control (implicit) Counter-Conditioning Reinforcement Management
24. NON-ABUSIVE PARENTING. Instruction and discussion of children developmental levels, discipline vs. punishment, and positive and negative reinforcement of behavior, followed by introductory skills-building.	Collaboration Self-efficacy Counter-Conditioning Reinforcement Management
Maintenance:	
25. RELAPSE-PREVENTION / BUILDING SUPPORTS. Personal reflection exercises and discussion about precursors to violence or coercion. Development of individual action plan for dealing with precursors, set-backs or relapse. Identification of personal and community resources for support. Visit from program graduate. Group revisitation of relationship/safety plan and final review of plan by group leaders. Administer Research Instruments and Program Evaluation.	Self-Liberation Helping Relationships
26. CONCLUSION: SELF-REFLECTION AND CLOSURE. Reflection by clients on changes made, current values, future goals, and plans to achieve them. Feedback from group members and leaders. Distribution of diplomas. Client evaluation of helpfulness of group and suggestions for improvement.	Self-efficacy Collaboration Self-Liberation Reinforcement Management

Table 2. Montgomery County APP Abuser Intervention Program Cognitive-Behavioral Gender
Reeducation Version Session Outline

Session Title	HANDOUT/*FILM*
1-2. INTRODUCTION/GOAL SETTING	Introductions and Goals (Program Philosophy and Purpose Contract/Ground Rules Introduction to Goal Setting and "Taking Care of Myself")
2. CONSEQUENCES OF DOMESTIC VIOLENCE	Costs and Payoffs for Abusive Behavior *FILM* Taking Responsibility for Abuse
3. CYCLE OF VIOLENCE/ TIME OUT	Cycle of Violence Calming Down Time Out
4. ANGER/ SAFETY PLANNING	*Deck the Halls* Anger Journal Personal Safety Plan
5. RECOGNIZING ABUSE/ TYPES OF ABUSE	Abuse Behavior Inventory Types of Abuse
6. AWARENESS WHEEL/SELF TALK	Awareness Wheel Self-Angering Thoughts/Combating Beliefs Held by Men who Batter Positive Self-Talk
7-8. CULTURAL INTEGRATION IN A CHANGING WORLD/ CHANGING MALE ROLE	*Men's Work Part I*
9. CULTURAL CHANGE IN RELATIONSHIPS	UN Declaration of Human Rights
10-11. POWER AND CONTROL/ EQUALITY	*Men's Work Pt II* Power and Control wheel Equality Wheel
12. SUBSTANCE ABUSE/ MANAGING STRESS	Substance Abuse Self-Questionnaire Alcohol and Domestic Violence Calming Down/Breathing Progressive Relaxation
13. SELF-EVALUATION	Evaluating Gains, Goal Setting and Feedback
14. GOAL SETTING	Goals
15. CYCLE OF VIOLENCE/ TIME OUT	Cycle of Violence Calming Down Time Out
16. FAMILY HISTORY	Family Tree Exercise
17-18. COMMUNICATION: SPEAKING SKILLS	Basic Guidelines for Speaking Feeling Wordlist Assertive/Aggressive/Non-Assertive
19-20. LISTENING	Basic Guidelines for Reflective Listening Non-verbal Barriers to Communication

	Guidelines for Fair Fighting Words Which Enhance Communication
21-22. CONFLICT RESOLUTION	6 Step Program for Resolving Conflict
23-4. PARENTING	Effects of Domestic Violence on Children Char. Behaviors of Children Who Witness Children of Divorce Children Learn What They Live Film: *It's Not Always Happy at My House*
25. RECOVERING FROM ABUSE/EMPATHY	
26. CONCLUSION/SELF-EVALUATION	Evaluating Gains, Goal Setting and Feedback for terminating members and those continuing next cycle Diploma/Letters

Table 3. Demographic Characteristics

	English-Speaking			Spanish-Speaking			English vs Spanish
	CBT (n = 175)	SOC (n = 200)	F	CBT (n = 106)	SOC (n = 47)	F	F
Age	35.4 (10.4)	36.6 (9.9)	1.08	33.3 (8.4)	31.4 (7.0)	1.33	9.90**
Education	13.0 (3.3)	12.5 (4.1)	1.88	8.22 (4.8)	8.9 (4.8)	.57	114.10***
Partner's Age	32.9 (10.2)	34.2 (9.6)	.96	31.9 (7.3)	28.6 (6.6)	4.89*	6.29*
Partner's Education	13.4 (2.4)	13.7 (2.3)	.65	9.4 (4.2)	10.0 (3.5)	.52	118.81***
			X^2			X^2	X^2
Referral source			4.05			5.56	4.06
Criminal court	54.7%	54.6%		59.6%	53.5%		
Civil order	36.6%	34.5%		36.4%	34.9%		
Juvenile court	1.7%	2.1%		2.0%	4.7%		
Pretrial referral	4.1%	2.1%		2.0%	2.3%		
Self-referred	2.9%	6.7%		0%	4.7%		
Multiple admissions	14.0%	10.6%	1.00	4.0%	11.6%	2.97	3.82
% Employed fulltime	45.9%	55.8%	3.01	28.0%	30.8%	.08	8.55**
Men's Ethnicity			2.64			5.16	303.58***
White/Cauc	29.9%	29.6%		2.0%	0%		
Black/African-Amer.	45.5%	45.5%		0%	0%		
Latino	14.4%	11.1%		96.0%	93.0%		
Asian Amer.	3.6%	5.3%		0%	0%		
Native Amer.	1.2%	0.5%		1.0%	0%		
Other	5.4%	7.9%		1.0%	7.0%		
% Immigrants	23.4%	27.5%	.81	76.4%	72.3%	.29	111.26***
% Currently in relationship	48.2%	43.9%	.52	69.8%	30.2%	1.77	.21
Marital Status			5.17			2.34	4.17
Never married	25.6%	20.4%		22.2%	26.2%		
Married/separated	28.7%	32.3%		36.4%	23.8%		
Married/living together	28.7%	31.7%		29.3%	38.1%		
Not married/living together	9.1%	5.9%		7.1%	7.1%		
Divorced	6.7%	5.9%		5.1%	4.8%		
Widowed	1.2%	3.8%		0%	0%		
% with children	73.4%	66.5%	1.67	79.0%	82.9%	.23	4.57*

*p < .05; **p < .01; ***p < .001.

Table 4. Lifetime Intimate Partner Violence

	English-Speaking			Spanish-Speaking			English vs Spanish
	CBT (n = 175)	SOC (n = 200)	F	CBT (n = 106)	SOC (n = 47)	F	F
CTS – Men's report							
SP – Psyc. Agg.	3.67 (2.10)	3.97 (1.98)	1.90	2.76 (2.10)	2.65 (2.14)	.08	26.28***
SP – Phys. Agg.	2.23 (2.26)	2.13 (2.09)	.17	1.34 (1.61)	1.30 (1.81)	.02	15.80***
SP - Injury	1.09 (1.33)	1.09 (1.30)	.00	.55 (.87)	.53 (.81)	.01	18.97***
SP – Sex. Coerc.	0.29 (0.66)	0.28 (0.54)	.02	.19 (.50)	.19 (.40)	.00	2.55
PS – Psyc. Agg.	4.54 (2.37)	4.82 (2.25)	1.28	3.50 (2.70)	4.08 (2.84)	1.17	15.91***
PS – Phys. Agg.	2.37 (2.53)	2.35 (2.30)	.01	1.53 (1.88)	1.89 (2.37)	.78	8.83**
CTS – Women's report	(n = 41)	(n = 38)		(n = 13)	(n = 7)		
PS – Psyc. Agg.	6.18 (3.30)	6.65 (3.45)	.38	7.50 (3.06)	4.50 (4.65)	2.40	.23
PS – Phys. Agg.	5.83 (4.80)	6.82 (4.79)	.67	9.22 (3.36)	6.67 (5.01)	1.75	3.16
PS - Injury	3.14 (2.45)	3.12 (2.48)	.00	4.78 (2.44)	4.29 (2.21)	.17	4.43*
PS – Sex. Coerc.	2.31 (3.09)	2.14 (2.90)	.04	6.27 (2.10)	5.00 (3.11)	1.08	19.93***
SP – Psyc. Agg.	3.84 (3.60)	3.78 (3.93)	.00	6.71 (3.95)	5.80 (4.09)	.15	4.37*
SP – Phys. Agg.	1.88 (3.64)	2.07 (3.84)	.02	9.33 (3.74)	8.57 (4.39)	.14	40.30***
DAS (Women's report)	(n = 58)	(n = 65)		(n = 20)	(n = 10)		
	4.66 (3.51)	4.83 (2.92)	.09	4.65 (3.51)	3.00 (3.20)	1.56	.96

*p < .05; **p < .01; ***p < .001. Note. SP = Self-to-Partner; PS = Partner-to-Self; Psyc.Agg. = Psychological Aggression; Phys. Agg; = Physical Aggression; Sex.Coerc. = Sexual Coercion; DAS = Danger Assessment Scale.

Table 5. Psychopathology and Trauma History

	English-Speaking			Spanish-Speaking			English vs Spanish
	CBT (n = 175)	SOC (n = 200)	F	CBT (n = 106)	SOC (n = 47)	F	F
PAI – Borderline traits	20.77 (11.12)	21.48 (11.03)	.00	20.17 (10.49)	19.55 (10.82)	.15	.65
PAI – Antisocial traits	14.16 (8.26)	15.05 (8.21)	.30	15.83 (6.59)	17.66 (7.02)	4.44*	12.15**
PAI - Suicidality	3.17 (3.69)	2.81 (3.37)	1.93	3.62 (2.99)	3.70 (3.33)	.43	3.18
PAI – Positive impression management	16.65 (5.16)	16.03 (5.10)	1.21	18.15 (5.28)	18.83 (4.59)	.46	14.27***
PAI – Infrequent responses	4.63 (3.44)	4.71 (2.91)	.05	6.37 (3.09)	5.70 (2.82)	1.28	20.65***
AUDIT	3.46 (5.18)	3.45 (3.83)	.00	4.73 (5.39)	3.56 (4.68)	1.33	3.53
Drug Abuse	.99 (1.32)	.90 (1.14)	.43	.09 (.33)	.11 (.31)	.06	57.00***
			X^2			X^2	X^2
Men's trauma history							
Child verbal abuse	38.5%	42.0%	.39	22.7%	8.0%	2.59	14.37***
Child physical abuse	31.5%	31.3%	.00	29.5%	27.0%	.08	.29
Child sexual abuse	14.9%	19.0%	.92	6.1%	4.0%	.15	7.54**
Witnessing IPV	21.2%	20.7%	.01	13.8%	4.0%	1.77	4.35*
Women's trauma history	(n = 51)	(n = 70)		(n = 26)	(n = 11)		
Child verbal abuse	35.3%	44.9%	1.13	23.1%	27.3%	.07	3.31
Child physical abuse	19.6%	27.1%	.92	46.2%	40.0%	.11	5.69*
Child sexual abuse	9.8%	23.2%	3.64	19.2%	9.1%	.59	.03
Witnessing IPV	26.5%	45.7%	4.51*	26.9%	54.5%	2.59	.09
Previous DV	14.6%	23.5%	1.42	30.8%	36.4%	.11	2.53

*p < .05; **p < .01; ***p < .001. Note. PAI = Personality Assessment Inventory; AUDIT = Alcohol Use Disorders Identification Test.

Table 6. Effect of Treatment Type on Desistance from Violence

Outcome	Variable	B	SE B	Exp (B)	Sig.	NR^2	-2LL	Model X^2	df	Sig.	% Cor.
XPOPSY						.002	399.2	.45	2	ns	58.2
(n = 294)	Treatment	.05	.25	1.05	ns						
	Language	.18	.26	1.20	ns						
XPOPHY						.004	283.94	.69	2	ns	81.5
(n = 297)	Treatment	.03	.32	1.03	ns						
	Language	-.25	.33	.78	ns						
VFUPSY						.062	106.84	4.01	3	ns	67.4
(n = 91)	Treatment	.93	.49	2.54	ns						
	VFUTIME	.02	.07	1.02	ns						
	Language	.36	.54	1.44	ns						
VFUPHY						.212	65.24	11.53	3	.009	83.9
(n = 91)	Treatment	1.50	.74	4.50	.042						
	VFUTIME	-.24	.11	.78	.025						
	Language	1.30	.84	3.67	ns						
VFUINJ						.329	27.43	10.84	3	.013	94.3
(n = 91)	Treatment	19.25	6386.92	2.3E+008	ns						
	VFUTIME	-.38	.22	.68	ns						
	Language	.79	1.20	2.19	ns						
VFUPHY (English)						.252	50.94	10.83	2	.004	81.3
(n = 67)	Treatment	2.01	.85	7.46	.019						
	VFUTIME	-.22	.11	.80	.048						

NOTE. NR^2 = Nagelkerke R squared; -2LL = -2 log likelihood; % Cor. = percentage correctly classified; XPOPSY = man's self-report on the CTS at post-treatment of the presence or absence of any psychological aggression toward his partner in previous 6 months; XPOPHY = man's self-report on the CTS at post-treatment of the presence or absence of any physical aggression toward his partner in previous 6 months; VFUPSY = victim's report on the CTS at follow-up of presence or absence of psychological aggression in previous 6 months; VFUPHY = victim's report on the CTS at follow-up of presence or absence of physical aggression in previous 6 months; VFUINJ = victim's report on the CTS at follow-up of injury in the previous 6 months; VFUTIME = length of time between onset of group and victim follow-up.

Table 7. Effect of Treatment Type on Assumption of Responsibility

	English		Spanish			
	CBT (n = 104)	SOC (n = 108)	CBT (n = 37)	SOC (n = 16)	F	Sig.
Change in URICA	.19 (.68)	.11 (.77)	.16 (.76)	.21 (.83)		
Treatment type					.01	*ns*
Language					.11	*ns*
Treatment X Language					.30	*ns*

Table 8. Effect of Treatment Type on Working Alliance

	CBT	SOC	CBT	SOC	F	Sig.
	(n = 21)	(n = 77)	(n = 11)	(n = 1)		
TW8TOT	48.1	56.3	70.4	52.0		
	(10.4)	(13.8)	(8.0)			
Treatment type					.56	*ns*
Language					1.72	*ns*
Treatment X Language					3.74	*ns*
	(n = 34)	(n = 63)	(n = 13)	(n = 27)		
TW16TOT	51.5	60.2	74.1	64.7		
	(9.2)	(13.6)	(8.6)	(9.1)		
Treatment type					.02	*ns*
Language					35.68	.000
Treatment X Language					15.85	.000
	(n = 8)	(n = 51)	(n = 11)			
CW8TOT	61.6	64.3	67.6			
	(8.8)	(11.2)	(9.1)			
Treatment type					.43	*ns*
Language					1.47	*ns*
Treatment X Language						
	(n = 28)	(n = 67)	(n = 13)	(n = 23)		
CW16TOT	62.0	62.8	74.7	76.5		
	(10.3)	(14.3)	(6.5)	(7.8)		
Treatment type					.27	*ns*
Language					28.34	.000
Treatment X Language					.04	*ns*

NOTE. TW8TOT = Therapists' rating of working alliance at Session 8; TW16TOT = Therapists' rating of working alliance at Session 16; CW8TOT = Clients' rating of working alliance at Session 8; CW16TOT = Clients' rating of working alliance at Session 16.

Table 9. Effect of Treatment Type on Group Cohesion

	CBT	SOC	CBT	SOC	F	Sig.
	(n = 7)	(n = 43)	(n = 10)			
GC8EMOT	8.3	7.7	7.4			
	(1.0)	(1.4)	(1.6)			
Treatment type					1.03	ns
Language					1.73	ns
Treatment X Language						
GC8TASK	8.4	8.2	7.7			
	(0.5)	(1.0)	(1.3)			
Treatment type					.33	ns
Language					2.24	ns
Treatment X Language						
	(n = 22)	(n = 31)	(n = 13)	(n = 23)		
GC16EMOT	7.4	7.3	7.9	8.4		
	(1.6)	(2.1)	(1.7)	(0.9)		
Treatment type					.22	ns
Language					4.96	.029
Treatment X Language					.85	ns
GC16TASK	7.7	7.8	8.5	8.3		
	(1.7)	(1.6)	(1.1)	(1.2)		
Treatment type					.03	ns
Language					3.62	ns
Treatment X Language					.08	ns

NOTE. GC8EMOT = Clients' rating of emotional group cohesion at 8 weeks; GC8TASK = Clients' rating of
task group cohesion at 8 weeks; GC16EMOT = Clients' rating of emotional group cohesion at 16 weeks;
GC16TASK = Clients' rating of task group cohesion at 16 weeks.

Figure 1. Men's Self-Reported Psychological Aggression at Post-Treatment

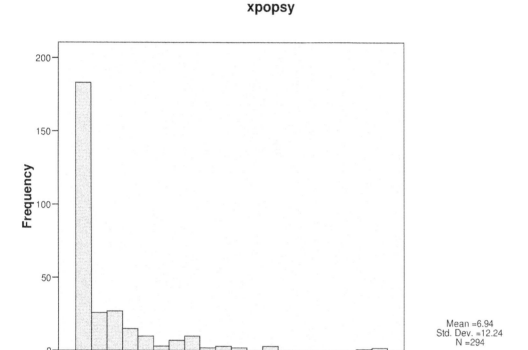

Mean =6.94
Std. Dev. =12.24
N =294

Figure 2. Men's Self-Reported Physical Aggression at Post-treatment

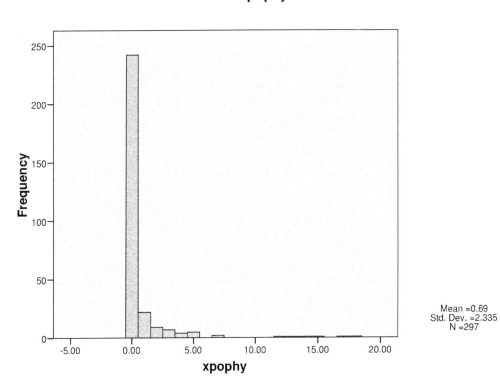

Figure 3. Victims' Report of Psychological Aggression at Follow-up by Treatment & Language

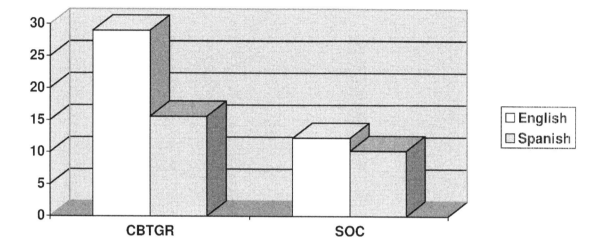

Figure 4. Victims' Report of Physical Aggression at Follow-up by Treatment & Language.

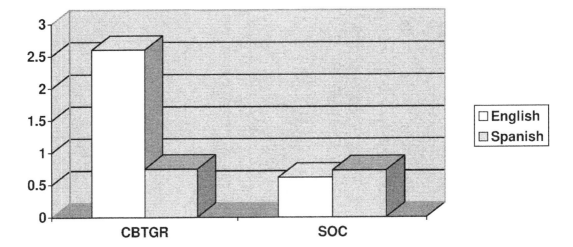

Figure 5. Victims' Report of Injury at Follow-up by Treatment & Language.

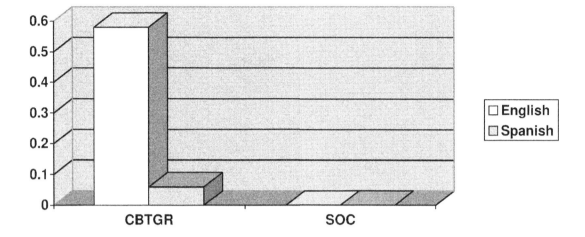

Figure 6. Victims' Report of Psychological Aggression at Follow-up.

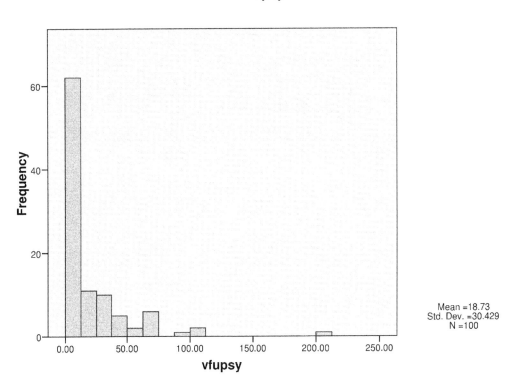

Figure 7. Victims' Report of Physical Aggression at Follow-up.

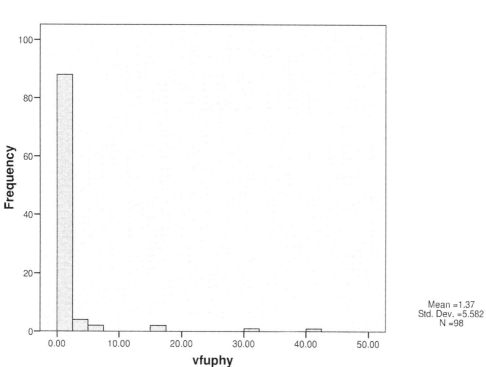

Figure 8. Victims' Report of Injury at Follow-up.

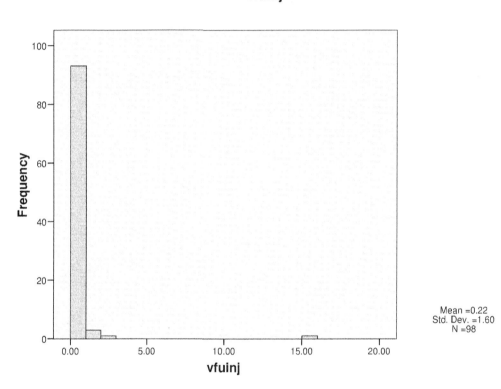

Figure 9. Victims' Report of Physical Aggression at Follow-up by Treatment Type & Men's Initial Stage of Change.

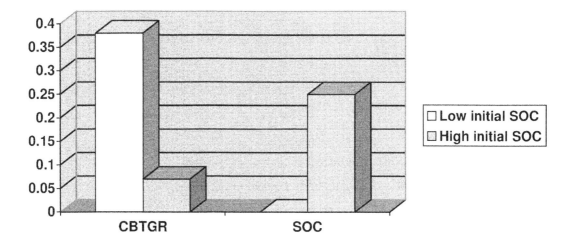

Appendix A

Therapist Adherence Items

Ideally, therapists in the SOC/MI condition should score **high** on each of the SOC/MI items and should score **low** on each of the CBTGR items.

Conversely, therapists in the CBTGR format should score **high** on each of the CBTGR items and should score **low** on each of the SOC/MI items.

SOC/MI Condition

- **Counselors expressed empathy for clients' experience.**
- **Counselors made use of open-ended questions.**
- **Counselors made reflective statements.**
- **Counselors briefly summarized what clients were saying and then explored further with the clients.**
- **Counselors encouraged reflection and questioning on the part of clients.**
- **Counselors focused on clients' values and motivations.**

CBTGR Condition

- **Counselors presented reasons why clients should change.**
- **Counselors adopted the role of the expert.**
- **Counselors focused on clients' behavior.**
- **Counselors confronted clients about abusive behavior.**
- **Counselors encouraged a change of controlling and abusive behavior.**
- **Counselors appealed to external authority, including therapists, society and the legal system, to facilitate client acceptance of the harmfulness of abusive behavior.**

CPSIA information can be obtained at www.ICGtesting.com
Printed in the USA
LVOW03s1939190815

450759LV00014B/362/P